THE MICKEY MANTLE STORY

THE
Mickey Mantle
STORY

AS TOLD TO *Ben Epstein*

FOREWORD BY *Casey Stengel*

ILLUSTRATED
WITH PHOTOGRAPHS

HENRY HOLT AND COMPANY
NEW YORK

Foreword

If someone asked me to list my top ten thrills in baseball, you can bet my first look at Mickey Mantle would have to be up there pretty high.

I had my first peek at Mickey at a Yankee special instruction camp in the early spring of 1950. He could do everything—run, throw, bat from both sides with power. When I saw him, my thoughts flashed back to many other great players I had seen breaking in, and I had to rate him up near the top with the very best of them all.

When we opened the regular Yankee spring training that year in St. Petersburg, I guess I talked as much about Mantle as I did about the Yankees who were out there on the ball field. It took a long time to forget what I had seen in Phoenix that spring.

Next winter the writers saw for themselves and they knew right off I hadn't been selling them any line. I could stop talking then. They were seeing for themselves. Mantle made the Yankees that season. Had to drop down to Kansas City for a spell during the season, but no one ever had any doubt he would be back.

Among the writers no one followed Mantle more closely than Ben Epstein. They tell me any time that spring Benny didn't mention Mantle in the first paragraphs of his story, the office would refuse to pay the Western Union charges on his copy. Maybe so or maybe not, but Benny got to know as much about Mickey as anyone connected with our camp.

And now he's putting it all down in a book as Mickey said it.

I thought I knew a lot about Mantle, but I know a lot more now after reading this book. And you're going to enjoy it all the way.

CASEY STENGEL

Contents

Introduction

Comment had simmered down to small talk in the Yankees' Soreno Hotel press quarters in St. Petersburg, Florida, following a spring exhibition game late one afternoon in March of 1950.

Casey Stengel, still regarded as a managerial freak despite his astounding 1949 championship bombshell, excused himself for a dinner date with general manager George Weiss. As usual, trade rumors mixed with the trade winds and Stengel muttered something about dovetailing his denials with those of the brass.

Most of the New York reporters also had retired to their typewriters. The stories, in those days, chiefly concerned the condition of Joe Di Maggio's heels and speculations about whom the Yankees would deal and for what.

Those remaining included club officials, visiting scribes, and baseball people in general.

Pitching coach Jim Turner, nursing a beer, contemplated the promise of a little blond left-handed rookie from Astoria, Long Island, one Eddie (Whitey) Ford. Catching coach

Bill Dickey, through "learning his experience" to Yogi Berra for another day, searched the trays for a stray sardine, his favorite hors d'oeuvre.

Some one wondered how much longer Di Maggio's legs could take it and if and when the Clipper called it quits, "Who in the world could possibly replace him? Without Joe, the Yankees will be without pennants."

There was a moment of silence and then from the corner of the room: .

"If you ask me, and nobody did, I would say the Yankees will be a long way from dead if Di Maggio holds out another year . . . I think we got the man."

The remark, said slowly and barely audibly, all but transfixed the listeners who stared at the speaker as if he were —well, had lost all of his marbles.

I laughed. "Tom, you sound as if you've had one too many for the road."

Tom was and is Tom Greenwade, a Yankee scout who dropped in to check on some of his finds. He's a long and lean Missourian who started out somewhere in the Northeast Arkansas League years ago as a player, manager, and subsequently a gent paid to appraise the bush talent for the majors.

Greenwade grinned. "Nope, you're wrong. I haven't tasted a thing but water since I've been in this room and I'm not hitting the road. I'm spending the night in St. Pete."

"Then, you're smoking stronger weeds lately or else you're kidding. Who's this Hall of Famer that's gonna pick up the slack left by Di Maggio?" It was a question put to him on behalf of the audience.

Tom's grin grew in a smile. He lighted a cigarette, took a long drag, and made the usual sign to the bartender.

"I want you to remember this name—Mantle. That's right, like the wood or stone over a fireplace." Noting he had the boys in the palm of his hand, Greenwade began to milk his audience.

"His first name is Mickey and his second name is Charles. He's only eighteen now and is going to play shortstop for Joplin this season. He's got more ability than any kid I ever saw and, go ahead, and get the laughs out of your system, before I go on."

The boys (except Turner and Dickey, who had seen Mantle at the Phoenix school the previous February) got the laughs out of their systems and Tom continued.

"This Mantle is a switch-hitter with home run power from either side. As a runner, he can fly. He has a powerful arm. It's wild but can be tamed. He's close to six feet, weighs one hundred and eighty pounds, and will be bigger.

"Found him in Oklahoma. In my opinion, he could be converted into a center fielder and, with luck, should be in the Yankee Stadium within two years. Remember the name —Mickey Mantle."

Mantle, as a fawning baseball world now knows, sensationally and spectacularly leaped beyond the dreams of the prophetic Greenwade. Mickey zoomed to the Yankees in one year, declined for a one-month refresher at Kansas City, and at the age of twenty, ably filled the yawning Di Maggio vacancy as the Yankees won their fourth straight World Series the past season.

Today, the game's most authoritative pundits, from Branch Rickey on down, hail Mickey, barring injury, as baseball's next super star. Indeed, several of the better-known bards have predicted that the season isn't too far off when he'll lead the majors in batting percentage, home runs, runs batted in, and total bases—slugdom's Grand Slam.

Bewildered and flabbergasted by it all, a dazed Mantle feels that the fans deserve some kind of a reply. And, mainly, because he asserts he's not another Ty Cobb or Tris Speaker or Di Maggio and never will be. He's just another guy who likes to play baseball and who got a lot of lucky breaks to make it possible.

Here's his story.

BEN EPSTEIN

THE MICKEY MANTLE STORY

1

Born for Baseball

I was born and bred to be a big league baseball player, preferably with the New York Yankees.

From the very minute the doctor told Dad, "You've got that son, Mutt," the plan for my future went into automatic operation. In fact, the blueprints had been drawn and, rumor has it, advertised months before delivery.

All I had to do was just enter the world as a boy. That's all.

Sixty seconds after my first squall on October 20, 1931, in Spavinaw, Oklahoma, I had been named in honor of Mickey Cochrane, then the star catcher for the Philadelphia Athletics, my dad's idol.

Mama says Dad showed me a baseball before I was twelve hours old, and it almost broke his heart when I paid more attention to the bottle. I can assure you this went on for quite a spell, but my dad wouldn't give up. He figured, Grandpa Charley recalled, "Mickey shows signs of being a slow starter."

Well, it didn't turn out that way. Things moved faster

than even my dad ever dreamed. Personally, I regard it as a miracle hastened by the greatest kind of breaks.

At the age of nineteen, I started the 1951 season for the Yankees in right field. And it's right here on Dad's chart that I should have been breaking in at Beaumont, with whom the Yankees had a working agreement in the Class AA Texas League.

Come to think of it, we (Dad and I) asked for the Beaumont assignment. And you can imagine our happy amazement, yet frightening reaction, to Casey Stengel's reply.

"What's the matter, son? Ain't the Yankees good enough for you? I got a hunch you're a little bit better than a road apple and, if you don't mind, I'm gonna keep right on looking at you."

I didn't mind and I still pinch myself to believe that, at twenty-one, I've been a member of the world-champion Yankees for two seasons. That is, if you don't count that month in 1951 when strike-outs, unbecoming to the bushiest sand-lotter, sent me to the Kansas City farm.

But I don't believe and never will believe that I'm another Ty Cobb, Tris Speaker, or Joe Di Maggio and whomever they're comparing me with. Incidentally, I learned to respect Di Mag, as great a guy as he is a player, and I'll tell you why later in this story.

Frankly, I'd settle to become as good an outfielder as are two of my teammates, Gene Woodling and Hank Bauer. And there are a gang of others around today, too, and if I had my choice among those on other clubs I'd possibly pick Dom Di Maggio.

About this switch-hitting. The popular question is: "Which side is it more natural, or easier, to hit from?" Here's the answer.

It's equally as easy (or tough) for me from either side. It feels the same. And you don't have to be a physical whiz (as some people think) to do it. Anybody can switch-hit if he starts early enough and works at it.

I started when I was five years old, thanks to the insistence of my dad who actually mapped out the experiment before I was born. His theory was that a player who could swing from both sides had a better chance of sticking around, because the percentages favored one against left- and right-hand pitching. It's as simple as that.

I think it's about time to introduce Dad, who died at the age of forty in May, 1952. He was Elven C. (Mutt) Mantle, who labored all his short life in the lead and zinc mines around Spavinaw, Picher, and Commerce, Oklahoma, to support his family and to realize his life's ambition: to make me a professional baseball player.

Thank God, he was able to see me in fourteen innings of World Series play (up to the time my right knee buckled in the second game against the Giants in the 1951 series) before he passed away. I wish he'd been around for the 1952 series . . . I saw him every day, though . . . and, well, I think you understand how I feel about it.

Let me tell you about the rest of my family. There's Mama, Mrs. E. C. (Lovell) Mantle; my sixteen-year-old twin brothers, Ray and Roy, a pair of all-around athletes; my fifteen-year-old sis, Barbara; Larry, an eleven-year-old little devil better known as Butch; and me. They're all crazy about baseball except Barbara, whose first and last sports love is football. Maybe it's because she's a cheer leader for Commerce High.

My wife, the former Merlyn Johnson of Picher, became Mrs. Mickey Mantle in December, 1951. By the way, another switch hitter is expected sometime in March, 1953. And don't let me forget to tell you that it took some romantic switch-hitting before I could get her to stop in front of the preacher's house.

I owe everything, of course, to Dad, buried at the GAR cemetery between Commerce and Miami, the seat of Ottawa County about five miles down the highway. But there were others, many others, who took me up the ladder to the New York Yankees.

The late Barney Barnett of Baxter Springs, Kansas, must go down as Number Two in my line-up. He's the one who taught me the first tricks of competitive baseball while acting as manager, sponsor, and father of the Baxter Springs Whiz Kids. Before he died of cancer in the fall of 1952, he got me an off-season job with H. D. Youngman, Contractor, Inc., of Baxter Springs. Harold, that's Mr. Youngman, is—well—a second dad, just like Barney Barnett was.

It's take-your-pick the rest of the way. All I know is, I never would have made it without the help and advice of these fine people:

Tom Greenwade, the scout who signed me to a Yankee contract.

Casey Stengel, for his understanding during my crying jags. Yes, I've actually wept in the dugout.

Tommy Henrich, for his patient and invaluable outfield teachings. Tommy would say, "Just listen to me and watch Di Maggio." How right he was.

The batting tips from Johnny Mize (pick up a copy of *How to Hit*, written by the Big Cat, Henry Holt and Company). And Bobby Brown and Johnny Hopp, who would take me out to Yankee Stadium hours before game time and pitch to me. I wouldn't be at all surprised if Bobby isn't still doing it in Korea between his hospital chores as army doctor. Brown, of course, had to be repaid and you did it by pitching to him. I believe there isn't a player around who likes to hit better than Bobby. He'd swing at a baseball if he had to stand in snow up to his neck.

And more batting suggestions from Allie Reynolds, Vic Raschi, Johnny Sain, and Ed Lopat. I've learned that pitchers of the class of the Chief, Vic, John, and Lope are wonderful instructors. It's simple: They tell you the kind of stuff the opposing pitcher throws. That sort of information really pays off every once in a while. Sain, as you know, is pretty fair with the stick, and he could have made it as a first baseman as well as a pitcher.

Then there's that show-how from Bill Dickey, Frank Crosetti, and Jim Turner. Dickey knows plenty about how to hold and swing a bat. I guess the best way to straighten you out on that item is to say Bill is Stengel's chief trouble shooter in that department. I also understand Dickey rates as one of the best shots (trap, skeet, and in the field) in Arkansas. I'm going to surprise him one of these days by knocking on his Little Rock door and asking him to invite me for a walk through the woods. Lopat already warned me if I ever do. Ed said that Bill will "walk you unconscious."

The Crow (that's Crosetti) also can tell you a thing or two about hitting. He's sharp, and coaching at third is just one of his many duties, although I'd like to know who'll outsmart him at third. But as far as I'm concerned, Frank spots certain weaknesses in pitchers you'd never believe existed. And Crosetti is second to none about shortstopping and knowing what goes on the left side of the infield. They told me Joe McCarthy made Phil Rizzuto watch Crosetti from the bench for a month when he first broke in. Why, maybe, the Crow could have possibly developed me into a shortstop but—hold it—that's asking too much.

Even the pitching coach, Turner, can toss in an occasional batting tip. I suppose you always can stop Jim by asking him what he wants to forget most about Mize. The same goes for Sain. The record book says Mize hit three homers in single games against both of them. But John, who did it as a Yankee against the Tigers in Detroit in 1950, is capable of doing it to any pitcher, any time, up to the age of fifty—meaning he's got ten more years to go. So that excuses Turner, who declares that running and more running makes you a better hitter as well as a pitcher.

But let me give it to you from the beginning. From the cradle, to switch-hitting at tennis balls at the age of five, to parading down the main drag of Commerce (to me, Ott Chandler's drugstore and the Black Cat Café pack more glamour than Broadway), up through the seventh game of the 1952 series against the Dodgers in Ebbets Field and all the pressure and pleasure in between.

2

My Cap and Gown

Up to the age of five, all I know is what they told me. And it all adds up that Dad insisted on my being taught the positions on a baseball field before the ABC's. An old friend of the family once recalled (and he swore he wasn't kidding) Dad said George Washington became the first president of the United States because he could throw.

It sounded like a whopper to me, but Mama says she wouldn't be at all surprised if Dad had said it. He was that crazy about baseball. Although he never played it professionally, Dad was a member of every town and company team in northeast Oklahoma that would have him.

I wouldn't know too much about Dad's baseballing, but I'll guarantee you he could run. Do you know what he did at the age of thirty-eight? Mind you, that's after my first season at Joplin and after the Yankees picked me up in St. Louis in September, 1950, and rewarded me with a trip through the West.

Well, he challenged me to a race. I told him to act his age. Besides, he was all tired out, having just come home

7

from the mines. But he was darn serious—so serious that he made cracks about my being afraid he could beat me. Truthfully, the thought did strike me, but I was hooked and accepted the challenge.

So he staked out about 100 yards on the road, pointed out a wooden bridge as a finish line, and hollered, "Go." Remembering the write-ups saying I could really run, I decided to take it easy on the old man. I took off easily and then almost broke my neck before I managed to pass him a couple of yards before the end.

It preserved my record of never having lost a race in my life. The only reason for my so-called speed, I suppose, is that I come from a running family. On both sides. Mama said she also was a racer while in high school and never lost one, either.

Nope, I never went out for track because Commerce High didn't have room for it what with baseball, football, and basketball on the program. Besides, the fellows who played these sports were three-letter men.

Still, all the Mantles can run. It's inherited, you might say. I also have a hunch there's a Mantle around, maybe two of them, who can outrun me. They're Ray and Roy. They really can fly, particularly Ray, on a football field. The twins have yet to challenge me. They will, I'm afraid, any season now.

Frankly, I'm not looking forward to it. Because if I lose, I'll never live it down. Little brothers are wonderful so long as they're littler than you. They're an inch taller than I am now and soon will catch up with me in weight. And I'll never get used to the fact that my "little" brothers will be known as my bigger and younger brothers.

Fortunately for all the Mantles, Mama is the most sports-minded mother in the nation. She's all for the theory that competitive sports make you a better man and not because they develop muscle, either. You know what I mean.

She tells me I was named after Mickey Cochrane. The Charles is after my two grandpas, my mother's father and his father's father. My father said he'd agree to any second name just as long as I signed my first name, Mickey. So to keep peace in the family, I said it would be all right with me.

I believe I was probably the only baby in history whose first lullaby was the radio report of a play-by-play broadcast of a ball game. I know it sounds insane but my father actually barked (and that's the word) me to sleep listening to the Cardinal games. This is Cardinal territory, or it used to be anyway.

One night, Mama says, I awoke during the seventh-inning stretch. She pleaded with Elven, for heaven's sake, to please cut off that contraption and let me sleep.

"You got Mickey wrong, hon," said Dad. "I don't blame him for screaming. Mickey isn't sick or hungry. It's just that he knew that the situation called for a bunt instead of hitting away and, in my opinion, he's a lot smarter than the Cardinal manager."

It wasn't long after I had "second-guessed" a major league ball game that I received my first bullpen orders. I was old enough to start looking like a baseball player. So after supper one night, Mama dug up some old cotton cloth and sewed me a baseball cap—beak, button, and all.

Meanwhile, Dad kept buying dime baseballs and throwing them in my cradle. It got so that, Mama tells me, I slid around as if I were moving on ball bearings. One day, about the age of one, I accidentally caught one of the ten-cent things. And Mama recalls that Dad became so overjoyed he yelled, "I'll bet you Cochrane wasn't half that good at his age!"

I wouldn't know about that. But I do know that Cochrane was earning his pay with the A's about the time Dad said it. According to the records, Cochrane hit .349 in 122 games in 1931 and .357 the previous season. I've got a hunch that Gordon Stanley outhit me by, at least, 100 safety pins, at the age of one.

I heard so much about Cochrane as a baby that Mama says I could say Massachusetts before I could Oklahoma. As you already guessed, that's because Cochrane was born in Bridgewater, Massachusetts, on April 6, 1903, and Dad always did consider the date of Mickey's birth one of his favorite bedtime stories.

I have yet to meet Cochrane, after all these years. And it's my fault, too. Mama, Merlyn, and I were eating at Theodore's in New York City after one of the 1952 Series games when somebody told me Mickey was in the restaurant. Mama, excited over it, suggested that I go over and introduce myself.

"After all, you were named after him," Mama said, "and that certainly should be enough for a formal introduction." Mama was right and I really wanted to. But suddenly I was too bashful to go through with it. I guess if Dad had been around he would have dragged me over to Cochrane's table.

On my third birthday, or about that time, Dad decided the time had come for me to be completely outfitted. In rompers and dresses and cute little hats? Not so you could tell it. But in a baseball uniform, made out of baseball material.

The family didn't have the cash for such highfalutin'

clothes but Dad had the answer. He sacrificed the pants of his own baseball uniform. Mama had the needle and thread. The outfit appeared a little bulgy around the seat, but then children my age were still wearing sliding pads. You know, the kind you fold together with safety pins.

All the same, Dad paraded me around town like Sunday-go-meetin' day. He once tried to slip me into a prayer meeting all decked out like that, but Mama talked him out of it, explaining that the church didn't have any backstop or something like that.

3

Pitch and Switch

My first lesson in switch-hitting is easy to remember because it started on the day I entered first grade as a five-year-old. That also explains why I graduated from Commerce High at seventeen. That's the way it was in those days, although I've heard the parents forced it on the School Board in order to get the youngsters out of the house. The sooner the better.

I don't remember too much about my first day in school but I remember plenty about the first hours after it. Two people were waiting for me as I returned home to 319 Quincy Street, following my first day of education—Dad and Grandpa Charley. Neither of 'em paid the least bit of attention to the green elephant I had crayoned except that it reminded Dad that Cochrane caught for the Elephants. Or Athletics or Macks. He had taught me the club's nicknames long before I could say, "hungry."

What seemed to absorb all their interest were a couple of tennis balls, juggled by Dad, and a two-bit bat gripped by Grandpa Charley. Dad kept repeating to Grandpa Charley he didn't suppose the tennis balls would hurt me and Grandpa Charley supposed right along with him. Nobody, not even Dad, could have possibly figured this little meeting of the Mantles started the first step of my baseball career which in two weeks had the neighbors wondering if I wasn't double-jointed.

Dad's proposition went something like this:

"Mickey, let's go out into the yard. Grandpa Charley and I have thought up a new game. You take this bat and try to hit our pitches. Don't be afraid of getting hit because these tennis balls can't hurt you." He bounced one off my belly and went on.

"Here's where the fun comes in. When I'm doing the throwing (Dad was left-handed) you swing as you always did—right-handed. But when Grandpa Charley (who was right-handed) throws, I want you to turn around and swing left-handed."

Being left-handed, Dad demonstrated by taking a cut. "Swinging left-handed might be a little hard (Man, was that an understatement!) in the beginning but, go ahead, and see if you can do it, anyway."

As you can understand, I couldn't do it, anyway or anyhow or upside down and backward when right-handed Grandpa Charley did the chucking. Swinging left-handed, even with a toothpick, was strictly for other folks. After about fifteen minutes of this fun, I hollered to Mama for help. But all she said was that she knew it was crazy but, please, go along and humor the old man. Years later, I found out that Mama was in on the scheme all along.

Despite my protests, Dad and Grandpa Charley kept pouring it to me every afternoon. Then, all of a sudden, say, about after two weeks, I didn't mind. Especially after

I managed to hit one, left-handed, every now and then. The baby muscles began to respond to training.

Here's the point. Anybody can develop into a switch hitter if you start early enough. It's no different from learning how to write. Any kid, naturally left-handed, can be taught to write right-handed, if he starts out that way. I know that type of teaching is out of bounds in the grade schools today but it can be done.

My daily switch-hitting drills, from four in the afternoon to nine o'clock at night (supper came afterward) began to attract attention. The neighbors, naturally, began to wonder what it was all about, and after they found out they began to watch my progress. Particularly after Dad devised some "scoring" rules.

The game came, of course, after I had been thoroughly "broken in" and Dad and Grandpa Charley began winging them in with all the stuff they had. And stuff they had plenty of, since a tennis ball will curve three times as much as a baseball. Yes, it will, too.

If you're keeping score, here's the way it went. A ground ball, pop-up, and strike-out were outs. A line drive off the side of the house, double; off the roof, a triple; and one into the trees (in the adjoining lot) a homer. I'm probably the only kid who ever made his old man proud of him by breaking a window.

But more about switching. When I was about six or seven, several of my school pals would drop over and watch Dad put me through the paces. Two got interested. Their names were Leroy Bennett and Nick Ferguson, both of whom grew into great high school athletes at Commerce.

Dad was tickled to have them around and before long had them switching as good as the next one. Leroy even went a step further. Right-handed all the way, he began to throw with either hand and, believe me, before long he was just as good from either side.

That was all right for Leroy but not for me. Dad wouldn't allow it since he then was grooming another Mickey Cochrane and left-handed catchers, of course, are passé. Which reminds me I've often heard Bill Dickey (who I'm told was every bit as good as Cochrane) say being a left-handed catcher isn't as ridiculous as it sounds.

Leroy and Nick gradually drifted away from the Mantle proving grounds and I would have, too, if Dad hadn't been around. Yet, rewarding me for being a good boy, he frequently took me hunting and fishing with him. I don't mean to sound confusing, but I shoot from the right side.

In Dad's book, there only was one way I could be "bad." That's when I disobeyed instructions and batted right-handed against a right-handed pitcher. I did it at the age of ten catching for Doughit in the peewee division of the Gabby Street League.

This was my first year in baseball. Batting left-handed against a right-hand pitcher in one particular game, I struck out three straight times. So, in my fourth trip, I switched to the right. But before I got a chance to strike out from the right side against a right-hand pitcher I heard a familiar holler rolling out. It was Dad's, who was studying me from a distance because, I guess, he didn't want me to know he was peeking.

The voice, full of "boy-you're-in-for-it," ordered, "Go on home and don't you ever put on that baseball uniform again until you switch-hit like I taught you." It scared not only me but everybody else. I scooted home, told Mama all about it. She told me not to worry and said I'd be playing catch with Dad before supper. Mama had the dope but not before I promised I'd never "sneak-switch" again and I never did.

I'd like to say here, though, that Dad's forcing me to bat left-handed must never be considered cruelty or severe punishment. Because swinging from the left side never bothered me physically except during my first month. And then, as I said, it only was a matter of adjusting or training the muscles to do it. Now, it's natural and nothing else.

Maybe I'm jumping the gun a little in advising kids "how to become baseball players." First, let me make it clear I've got a long way to go in hoeing my own row. But I owe most of my success or whatever you want to call it by liking to play and, more important, by playing. All the books and coaching on the game aren't worth a hoot if you don't play —all the time. It's only then that the reading and teaching part begins to make sense.

But I wish Dad could have taught me how to keep from striking out. Let me remind you that my 111 strike-outs in 1952 broke Frankie Crosetti's Yankee record of 105 set in 1937. A baseball writer recently consoled me about strike-outs, pointing out that 1,330, the all-time record, is held by Babe Ruth. I guess I'll beat Ruth's mark in that department in half the time it took the Babe.

4

Just Growing Up

As a Peewee Leaguer, I was just about the peeweeist peewee in the county. I didn't weigh much more than a hundred when I started out in what you might call competitive baseball, and gained no more than fifteen pounds during the next three years.

As growers, the Mantles take their time and then, all at once, we sprout quicker than early June peas.

Although I stayed a runt, I branched out as a player, you might say. That is, when Dad was digging at the mines and busting up the jack separating the lead from the zinc, I'd try my hand at other positions. Not that I didn't like catching; I did, but curiosity or the desire to play all over the place got the best of me.

Besides, my head began to swell a little. Not only were the neighbors talking about that little squirt who could switch-hit, but they said I could run fast. "Too doggone fast for a catcher," they'd say. Of course, that was long before catchers like Yogi Berra could scat from first to third on a base hit to right field just like that.

Anyway, about the age of twelve and, I believe, while playing for Picher in the Junior Cardinal League, I talked the manager into letting me take a whirl at second base. Besides, the second baseman had the measles.

Naturally, Dad caught me "cheating" but surprise of surprises, he failed to lay down the law. Could be he figured I had better possibilities at some other spot. Chances are my running changed his opinion although he remained a Cochrane man to the day he died.

That's about the way it went in those days. At thirteen, I reached high school (my teachers must have been baseball fans) and Grandpa Charley passed away. That was in 1945.

We had moved out of the Commerce city limits by then but a wisecracker might ask, "How could you tell the difference?"

Dad swapped our house on Quincy Street (my tennis ball backstop) for some hogs and cows and chickens and a tractor for the right to farm 180 acres along the Neosho River. We rented the place mainly because Dad wanted to get Grandpa Charley, then a very sick man, away from the mines.

It was fun farming, particularly because it made it a lot easier to hunt and fish. I rode a horse to school, about ten miles from town. He sure was an understanding horse and didn't like school, either . . . just loved to "run away" with me on his back and start grazing around some fishing hole.

The crops were good, with the corn, wheat, and oats really yellowing up the land. Then it started to rain and rain and rain. Backwaters of the Neosho backed in, flooding practically all our acreage.

It bankrupted us. So much so that we had to quit the

place and move into a shack on the edge of Commerce. I've appreciated plumbing ever since.

Regardless of the family misfortunes, Dad worked day and night to guarantee our schooling and baseball for me. As a high school freshman, I pitched for Commerce in addition to the outside amateur play. I also "went out" for basketball and dreamed of playing football. I also began to get visions of playing in college. That's all the folks talk about in the fall in Oklahoma, anyway. Even in the bigger places like Oklahoma City and Tulsa you read about oil and hear about football.

I was much too little for football, and even if I were big enough it wouldn't have made any difference. Dad accepted the sport and thought it was all right—for other people. But not for little Mickey. And every time I'd as much as play that I was calling signals, he'd hush me up with the warning it would bust me up for baseball. You hear the same thing around any baseball office but put me down as neutral. I don't want to start any arguments but, if you ask me, the Yankee scouts aren't fond of it if they figure a fellow is a baseball prospect. Dad didn't mind basketball after they took the body-contact out of it, and he said it helped your wind, too.

Football nearly ruined my life, but don't let me get ahead of myself. At the time, however, I wouldn't take no for an answer in my desire to play football. About the only way I can say it is that football just gets you. My begging and pleading (and added weight as a sophomore) finally made Dad give in but he didn't hooray when he did. After all, I had everybody working on him including my coach, then Allen Wollard, now going places at Lawrence, Kansas, who's going to be heard from. (Allen named his baby after me, a cute little all-American born in November, 1952.)

So I became a member of the Commerce High School Tigers backfield. And I guess I was doing pretty good, too. I don't know about starring but I was more than satisfied. I was scoring for the House of Mantle! During one particular game after I got off a touchdown run, I spotted Dad yelling his head off. A teammate noticed it also while we lined up to take the kickoff and he kidded me about watching out about my punting, since Dad might get the idea of developing me into a switch-kicker. I kick right-footed.

It was about a week later during a scrimmage when it happened: the "scratch" which blew up into a mountain and spread all over the country. It has given me more physical pain and personal troubles than I believed possible. It bounced all the way to the United States Army Surgeon General in Washington and back again and, for all I know, it's still bouncing. And I guess nothing can be done about it.

But let's get back on the field. *I got kicked in the left shin.* I hardly noticed it. In fact, I rubbed it a little and got back in the scrimmage. Still, the pain didn't leave after a hot shower and I limped home. I brushed it off as a sprained ankle. Mamma soaked the shin in a bucket of hot water. That eased it some and I figured it would be O.K. after a night's rest. It worked before and I thought it would work again and then there was that little warning from Dad about not getting injured in football.

I didn't sleep; by morning the ankle had swelled to twice its normal size and turned a dirty blue. Dad's eyes rounded out like saucers when he saw it but he didn't bawl me out as I expected. Instead, he rushed me to the town doctor. The doctor didn't like the looks of it and said he couldn't diagnose it properly because there was no X-ray equipment in Commerce at the time.

But he did detect an infection and advised me to go to the Eagle Picher and Lead Company hospital in Picher where they could make a thorough examination. Dad put me in the car and off we went. And it was there where I learned, for the first time, that I suffered from osteomyelitis. The Picher doctor skipped the big word and explained it was a bone disease—one that didn't check easily. I soon learned how to spell it.

None of us, except the Picher doctor, realized the seriousness of it. When it finally dawned on me that possibly I would be forced to forget about baseball, hunting, and other sports, I thought I'd go crazy. Dad thought the same thing but never said a word. He didn't get panicky. He told me to hang on, then put me in the car, and drove me all the way to Oklahoma City. He already had made inquiries and learned that it was the best place in the state to go for treatment of the disease.

I'll never forget those two weeks in Oklahoma City. Penicillin every three hours for two solid weeks. And diathermy all the time. Every now and then, strange doctors would come in, take a look, and cloud up. There was even talk, I learned later, of amputation. It was that bad. But, thank God, treatments finally stopped the infection—temporarily. When they discharged me from the clinic with a lot of take-it-easy warnings, they gave me a present: a pair of crutches.

5

I'm a Big Boy Now

Hobbling around on crutches reminded me of a guy serving time in a chain gang. I felt as if I were going crazy—and fast. It was all because I wanted to play, any kind of sport, and couldn't. It's rough on a kid who has always been active.

People would look at me, ask about my condition, and wish me the best. And all they got for their troubles was a series of insults, studded, I'm afraid, with some plain and fancy cussing. I'd catch them shaking their heads in pity. Their sympathy only would upset me all the more. I just couldn't take it. How my family and friends took it, I'll never know.

Deep down, Dad was taking it much worse and, I might add, much more sensibly. He figured a "change" would snap the tension. And what a heavenly change it was. He showed me a couple of tickets (in the grandstand) to the 1946 World Series between the Red Sox and the Cardinals. St. Louis isn't much over 300 miles from Commerce.

I forgot every ache and pain and everything else while

watching the first two games in St. Louis when the Sox won the opener, 3–2, in ten innings on Rudy York's homer and the Cards won the second, 3–0, on Harry Brecheen's four-hit shut-out.

If someone would have told me that five years later I would have been with the Yankees and playing against these very same clubs and many of the same players in exhibitions and league competition, I would have laughed at the idea.

As I said, seeing such stars as Brecheen, Ted Williams, Stan Musial, Bobby Doerr, Howie Pollet, Dom Di Maggio, Country Slaughter, Tex Hughson, Terry Moore, and a gang of others is for a fourteen-year-old country boy the thrill of a lifetime. No ands, ifs, or buts about it.

On returning home, I ordered Mama to burn the crutches.

That very same fall I played football, basketball, and baseball with Commerce High and the following summer became the second baseman for Miami, Oklahoma, then in the Ban Johnson League.

What happened to my infected shin? It stayed infected but I managed to keep it under control, thanks to almost daily treatment. They've never stopped. Ask Dr. Sidney Gaynor, the Yankees' bone man who really knows how to keep osteomyelitis in an arrested state. But I continued to play. Between flare-ups, that is.

Right now I'd like to put in my two cents' worth about the Ban Johnson League. As far as I'm concerned it's the greatest amateur baseball organization of its kind in the world. It covers the tristate area (a radius of about 150 miles) of that territory embracing northeast Oklahoma, southeast Kansas, and southwest Missouri.

The clubs run from six to ten (according to the pocket-books of the sponsors, managers, and supporters) and have been operating as long as I can remember. I can't tell you too much about its origin, but it belongs in Cooperstown on its merits of fighting juvenile delinquency, if nothing else.

During the tail end of my first year with Miami in the B. J., I lined into a triple play, batting left-handed. We were playing Baxter Springs, managed by Barney Barnett. It was the luckiest "drive" I ever hit. Even though he "set" his right fielder in position to make the triple play, Barney seemed to like the way I connected with the ball, and asked Dad if he could have me for his Baxter Springs Whiz Kids for the 1948 season. Dad and Barnett were old friends, Barney being a ground boss himself and a "company" ball-player in his youth. Besides, Miami was going to drop out of the league.

Dad jumped at the offer. He knew that Barnett not only knew as much inside baseball as the next one, but was regarded as "boy's best friend." I can't say enough about that. Barney would and did spend his last dime and did everything but steal to outfit kids with baseball equipment. Barnett went even further than that. He roomed and boarded every kid who couldn't afford to stay elsewhere in his own house, a big two-story place in Baxter Springs. What did Barney get out of it? Well, here's what he told Ott Chandler before he died, "What you keep in this world is what you give it."

When I look back on it, I guess my two years under the coaching of Barnett were the happiest of my life. He reminded me of a year-round Santa Claus, just getting joy out of helping people. And come to think of it, I believe I never heard him make a single complaint to anyone. That is, if you scratch out a few squawks at an umpire. Even then, he'd apologize after the game was over. In a way, he had to, because he was forced to dig up the umps as well as the players. But the umps loved him as we kids did, but I don't believe you can say the same for the umps and managers in pro baseball.

Barney moved me to shortstop at the start of the 1948 season. Said I was wasting my arm as a second baseman. But the shift hit him with a serious problem. My "wasted" arm not only ruined about five first basemen but shortened the lives of three left fielders and two center fielders. I couldn't catch the grounders. Not too often, anyway. Yet Barnett said I was "his" shortstop because, of all things, "you won't quit on a ball even after you miss it." It turned out to be a valuable lesson. I don't quit on them but I still miss them.

As a Whiz Kid, we traveled in "big league" style, I thought. Besides Baxter Springs, the league's other Kansas towns included Coffeyville and Parsons, and our Missouri jumps (by car and bus and hitch-hike) were Joplin, Seneca, Alba, and Carl Junction. I often think of those towns while in the Yankee Stadium and, so far as baseball is concerned, have come to the conclusion that it's actually no different. The fields are smaller and the stands are bigger and that's about it.

My switch-hitting always seemed to interest Barney. And there were times when he thought I'd be a better over-all hitter if I stuck to one side. However, he was smart enough to tell me such discussions were strictly confidential since he didn't want Dad to think he was meddling. Frankly, Barnett figured I was a better right-hand batter or had more power from my "natural" side, anyway. I don't believe he ever changed his mind, either, no matter how far or hard I'd hit one left-handed. Which reminds me of a story I read during my first year with the Yankees which said I'd go farther as left-hand batter. It said drag-bunting from the left side would give me a big edge for an average. I don't think so and no Yankee official even as much as suggested it to me.

I'll never forget my most "profitable" night in Baxter Springs. Hit three homers. Somebody passed around the hat and dumped it in front of me in the clubhouse. All of us, including Barney, began counting the pennies, nickels, dimes, quarters, and half-dollars. It amounted to about $50. I was rich. Too rich, because it got around—too far around and I became poor again.

They heard about it in the Lucky Seven. That's our high school conference of Picher, Grove, Chelsea, Quapaw, Afton, Jay, Wyandotte, and Fairland besides Commerce. I know that adds up to nine schools but it's still the Lucky Seven. And the Lucky Seven let me have it—and I don't mean the money. They told me if I kept the fifty bucks, I would become a professional and become ineligible to compete in high school athletics. I had to return the money— or else.

So I turned it all back to Barney, who really wanted me to have it. He knew I wanted it and I'm not ashamed to say that my folks could have had plenty of use for it. The family was growing and, at the time, the price of lead and zinc was down. I know a few things about the metal market. It can be a lot more important than the comics to kids who know their bread depends on it. Barney squared me with the Lucky Seven by donating the money to charity.

Years later, during the 1952 football season to be exact,

I pulled the same rule on the twins—Roy and Ray. I promised them five dollars for every touchdown they scored. It got serious after the first five games when they scored about fifteen between them. I alibied that as much as I'd like to pay them I couldn't because it would brand them as pros and ruin their high school careers. Then I cited my old experience. They argued it wasn't the same thing. I hedged by telling them to come back with a ruling.

6

Taking the Yankee Pledge

I got my taste of being on a pennant winner during my first year at Baxter Springs. And, luckily, I haven't been on a loser since. That noise you hear is the wood I'm knocking.

Let's see. Baxter Springs won the Ban Johnson League pennants in 1948 and 1949. I also joined the Independence (Kansas) club of the Class D KOM League in June, 1949, and, sure enough, Independence came through. Joplin won the Western in 1950 and the Yankees, naturally, true to form, won the world championships in 1951 and 1952.

I didn't mean to get ahead of myself. Still, it's a good and profitable feeling to have been with six straight pennant winners. Stengel won't make me a bit sore if he keeps right on going for his fifth straight.

As a pro you get to keep the money and as a Yankee the pay-offs (and fatter ones) run right through the first week in October.

During my last year at Baxter Springs and my senior year in high school, Barney Barnett was booming me up to every

scout who would listen. I wouldn't be at all surprised if
Dad was in cahoots with him on the whole deal.

I didn't know it at the time, but during a trip to St. Louis
to take in a big league game, (Barney did it about twice a
year), he submitted my name to Bill DeWitt, then one of
the owners of the Browns. I never did hear from Mr. De-
Witt, though.

Barnett played no favorites, begging any and everybody
to give me a chance. He even prevailed upon Joe Becker,
Ban Johnson League president who also sidelined as a scout
for the Red Sox. However, Becker, who also is a good friend
of mine and who served as emcee at the banquet in my
honor on October 17, 1952 (Spartan Cafeteria, $2 per
plate), said Boston couldn't use me because they didn't have
any Class D farms.

Meanwhile, Dad had been doing a little shopping around
on his own. He said something about having met a Tom
Greenwade, a Yankee scout. I never did get it straight how
Greenwade heard about me. I believe that Johnny Sturm,
former Yankee first baseman who then managed Joplin,
tipped Tom I was worth a look but I'm not sure.

Greenwade told Dad he had time to size me up on Friday
night, May 16, 1949. Baxter Springs was scheduled to play
at Coffeyville. That was fine—except for one thing. I was
scheduled to graduate from high school that night and already had scratched myself from the line-up.

Dad straightened out the situation in nothing flat. He
rushed over to the school superintendent and gave him that
"chance-of-a-lifetime" routine. His speech not only got me
excused from the commencement but he also brought home
my diploma. On top of that, John Lingo who coached me

my senior year also decided to give the exercises a miss and go along with me.

So the whole family and coach John piled into the old jalopy and headed for Coffeyville.

I had a good night . . . three for five . . . single, double, and homer. I connected from both sides.

Greenwade didn't hurrah. He said he was going over to inspect somebody at Independence but would be back Sunday afternoon when Coffeyville played a return at Baxter Springs. We won, 8–0, and after the last out I jumped into our car to escape a rainstorm.

Two other persons who didn't want to get wet also were in the car—Greenwade and Dad. I'll never forget the thrill I received from Tom's first statement. He said it loudly so we could hear above the wind and rain whipping the car.

"Well, Mutt and Mickey," he drawled, "I'm ready to sign you to a Yankee contract."

I was speechless from excitement and Dad didn't say anything, either, for about a full minute. Yet, I knew he never was happier. He was grinning and his eyes shone like a brand new electric light.

After all this had sunk in, Tom continued, "I can't offer you much of a bonus because, well—I don't think you're worth a bonus. But I'm willing to give you a Yankee check for $1,100 if you sign this contract which will make you a member of the Independence ball club which will pay you about $140 per month until the end of the season.

We signed. Why did I sign for peanuts during a time when kids, a lot less known than myself, were getting fabulous bonuses? Well, I'll tell you why. Nobody offered me one. I'd have broken an arm reaching for a pen if I'd gotten an offer for as much as $5,000.

And the proposition didn't necessarily have to come from the Yankees. Let's be honest about it. Any club could have had me for a price. The only other club to approach me before the Yankees was the Cardinals. Runt Marr of St. Louis talked to me about a week before I saw Greenwade. Marr said he'd sign me but no bonus.

Of course, it turned out that my signing with the Yankees was the luckiest day of my life. But, at the time, how was anybody to know I'd be a member of the Yankees within two years. It's still a million-to-one shot that came in. I just hit the jackpot during spring training of 1951.

On the other hand, I knew Greenwade was right when he said I wasn't worth a bonus. I wasn't despite my write-ups as an "amateur star." Tom gave it to me straight. He then told me of the possibilities of being a Yankee. It sounded like a little too much butter at the time but, as it turned out, he wasn't kidding one bit.

That's when Greenwade started squeezing the green out of my system. He shipped me to a Yankee tryout camp at Branson, Missouri, where the instructors—Burleigh Grimes and Dutch Zwilling—had orders to package me up and send me to Independence. Grimes and Zwilling looked me over and had me feeling "like a Yankee" within a couple of days. Grimes is a funny guy and somebody said I should have seen him before he replaced Stengel as manager of the Dodgers.

7

I Never Left Home

Remember the old saying: "You can take the country boy to the city but you can't take the country out of the boy"?

That's me and that's the way I'm going to be—forever more.

I'm loaded with hayseed and aim to stay that way. Don't get me wrong. I'm not knocking the city way of life. But those big city apartments and town houses always struck me as foolishly paying your money to eat and sleep in a jail.

If I can't wake up in the morning, noon, or night without knowing I can cross a road for a mess of fish or walk down the pike a piece without flushing a covey of birds, I'm homesick.

And, to my mind, that's the only thing I don't like about pro baseball or any job for that matter. I knew from the minute I signed up that it was so long to my rod and gun until the off season. Why even a dog can forget you in six months.

I complained to Dad about it. He would ease my troubles

by saying that my "new earning power" would allow me to buy better outdoor equipment and such.

Dad also knew something I didn't tell him. I also was afraid to leave home. I guess there was no substitute for Mama's coffee and grits, among other things, and the thought of being away from the house for more than a day scared me hollow.

Actually, the KOM League covered the neighborhood, you might say. Miami, then in the league, was no farther away than the fancy grocery store. Carthage, Missouri, was only thirty-five miles from Commerce and Pittsburg, Kansas, about forty. The speedometer said Independence, Kansas, my home base, was seventy-five miles away from the Blue Goose, No. 1, the mine where Dad worked as a ground boss.

Still, I felt like a foreigner. Dad kidded me about not having to worry about losing my citizenship. He also promised he and the family would show up at the games every night no matter in what town we played. They darn near did it, too, and I'll bet there were times when he had to draw advances on his salary for the gas and oil and spares for the flats.

I guess I played shortstop for about a week before Harry Craft (who'll manage Kansas City in 1953) called me aside for my first bit of professional instruction. Having caught a few on the nose, I was all swelled up, listening to what a wow I was for seventeen and a half years old.

"Mickey," he said, "you'll never advance much higher than you are right now, Class D, if you don't learn to keep your head up when you return to the dugout at the close of an inning. You act as if you're ashamed of yourself. Yankees don't conduct themselves like that. Act like a champion and, someday, you might even play like one."

Craft spotted my most glaring weakness (except striking out) right from the beginning. I wasn't afraid of the crowds as long as I didn't have to look at the customers. Especially after I failed in the clutch at the plate or booted one or pulled a skull in the field. And I really came in with my share. So to get around it, I would double up like a worm on a fishing hook and sneak into the dugout.

"Straighten up," Craft would say, "nobody is going to arrest you because you made an error. Look at the big league box scores tonight and you'll note that some clubs committed more errors than we did." Sometimes I thought I couldn't straighten up with a broom stick in my back. Even today while I'm trotting to the bench my head is twisted to the left and jerked down as if I had a crick in my neck.

I'd give anything if I could shake off a bad day as Berra does but I guess I'm not geared like Yogi. Bob Kuzava is another guy who can take it, good or bad. For instance: His ice water showers in the final games of the last two World Series. Bobby Brown once kidded me that a course in philosophy would correct it but I told him Berra didn't study any philosophy.

"That's right," replied Brown. He then laughed. "But Yogi used to be my roomie on the road when we played for Newark in 1946. Maybe some philosophy rubbed off on him." I wouldn't know but I hope to be looking straight ahead, at least, within two more years—I hope. You should have seen me at Independence and Joplin. It got so the players from both teams used to greet me, "Hello, Jackknife."

I never could face folks if I was a side attraction, much less the center of it. I knew it from the time they talked into appearing in a senior high school play. And would you listen to the name of it: "Starring the Stars." They even sold tickets to it.

You guessed it—I folded up in the final rehearsal. I reported for the big show and that was on stage, too. But behind the curtain. I was the prompter and between prompts, read three chapters of *Goodbye, Mr. Chips.* The teacher never forgave me for running out on her. She said she thought I was a "good organizer."

Let's return to my comedy at Independence as we bounced around the KOM. I didn't know it then, but I picked up valuable pointers during my first half-year of pro ball that saved me a lot of trouble and embarrassment as a big leaguer.

Craft taught me the full meaning of hustle. I know it's old hat and you hear about the "ole hustle" until you're sick of it. But not the way you learned it from Harry. Here is an example: How many times have you seen a batter (even in the majors) barely crawl down to first base after popping out? I know it's almost a sure thing to be caught. So you think, "Why waste the energy?"

That doesn't go in Craft's book. Harry manages under the theory of taking advantage of that "sure shot" when and if it comes in. He declares that it's just such breaks that win pennants. Consequently, Harry orders players to run them out all the way. He even makes it interesting: "See how many bases you can reach before a pop-up is caught—or dropped or misjudged."

Personally, I always try for two and sometimes can make it "safe," and I could be the winning run in such a case. It's one of the reasons I hit .322 in 87 games at Independence. I got 101 hits in 314 trips, hit 15 doubles, 7 triples, 7 homers, and batted in 63 runs.

I hope I'm not kidding myself in believing these figures had a lot to do in winning me a trip to the Yankees' first school for farm prospects at Phoenix, Arizona, in February, 1950.

8

Come See Me, Boy

I was monkeying with a sledge hammer in the electrical shop of Blue Goose No. 1 when Dad dropped around one afternoon in November of 1949. He casually remarked something about Joe McCarthy who might do it in his third year as manager of the Red Sox.

"Wouldn't be at all surprised if McCarthy finally wound up on top next season," said Dad. "Anybody who loses out in a play-off to the Indians as he did in 1948 and losing out to the Yankees on the last day of the past season is certainly flirting with a pennant, to my way of thinking."

I nodded an agreeable uh-huh and Dad added easily, "By the way, Mickey, you got a postcard from Joe Payton today. They want you to drop around for an examination in a couple of weeks."

Dad let it sink in. He knew I knew all about Mr. Payton. I'd never had the pleasure of meeting him personally, but several of my friends who also had heard from him had discussed his sideline in my presence. Besides being a linotype operator on the Miami (Oklahoma) *Daily News-Rec-*

ord (whose managing editor, Mack Bartlett, is a pal of mine), Mr. Payton served on the Ottawa County Draft Board.

I'd like to put in here that Joe (I'm taking the liberty of using his first name because we got to see a lot of each other) rates as one of our county heroes. As Sergeant Joe Payton, he received a Meritorious Achievement Award fighting with the 466th Bombardment Group in World War II.

I had visions of being a gunner in one of those big flying jobs as I underwent my physical (the first of three) a couple of weeks later. But the draft board doctors didn't like the looks of that running sore on my left shinbone. Several days passed and then I received the news I had been listed 4-F. The service, I was told, wanted no part of osteomyelitis, then classified as a disease which exempts one from soldiering in any form.

Although I can truthfully say I never asked for a single favor or even as much as hinted toward a deferment, the 4-F tag worried me. The fact that I stacked up as a possible total disability case to the government and being a chronic sufferer for the rest of my life, well—imagine how you would feel if it happened to you. I was advised to continue taking shots and treatment if I hoped to "remain active." And so far, so good, but I hate to think about it.

After walking around in a trance for about a month, I gradually shook it off. The twins, as Commerce High freshmen, were beginning to make the teams and I spent practically all my time watching them and, I guess, acting as their publicity agent in the school paper—the *Tiger Chat*. Don't tell any of those New York sports writers but I used to be a member of the *Chat* Sports Department. I was written up in a big way in the October 15, 1952, edition. It started off with a big headline:

FORMER STUDENT STAR OF YANKEES IN SERIES.

And then it went on to say:

"Mickey Mantle, the name that electrified the baseball world and headed the sports news in the leading newspapers of the country, is a familiar name in the halls of Commerce High School because this is his alma mater. While the Yankees were in the big battle and crowds of 70,000 were being thrilled by spectacular playing, there was much tension and excitement in this remote scene. Many ears were turned to listen in on the performance of a home-town boy.

"It was a liberal education for most of the school during the ball games and the public address system was used as an opportunity to pipe activity into ordinarily dry math and history rooms. Mickey came home in time to see his former classmates play a winning football game with Picher, an old-time foe. *Tiger Chat* speaks for the entire school when we say, 'Welcome!' Commerce High School is proud that you belong to us."

Couldn't have been any better if I'd written it myself. And since I'm bragging, I'll also let you in on something else. I finished second in a county scholastic contest (that's journalism as well as readin' and writin', son), a feat that absolutely floored my English teacher, Miss Hazel Crosby. She made me enter because "I didn't like poetry." But the girl sitting in front of me (and over whose shoulder I peeked) sure did know her stuff.

I had determined to "remain active" regardless of the condition of my leg. So between meals and during my time-outs at the mine, I doubled up in my hunting, scrimmaged with the Tigers in basketball, and swung that sledge hammer.

And for the information of Lou Boudreau, who once wondered if I switch-hit with a sledge, the answer is no. Only from the right side, Lou, when I'm not in the rough.

I was going to be in the best possible shape during my first full season in the Yankee organization. It sure came in handy, too, because I heard from the front office weeks before I expected to.

Lee MacPhail, head of the farm system, wrote me in January, 1950, about some kind of a look-see school they were holding for the so-called "brighter" minor leaguers at Phoenix the following February and I had been chosen as one of the pupils. Frankly, I thought that was pretty good going for a fellow who had only a half-season of Class D under his belt.

We (referring to us green peas, including Jackie Jensen, then a pitching hopeful and Jim Brideweser, a shortstop like myself) just looked during our first day at Phoenix. There was plenty to see. Besides Stengel and Dickey and Crosetti and Turner, there were established stars around like Berra, Bauer, and Cliff Mapes, all of whom were listed as "instructors."

I read stories later where Happy Chandler, then the commissioner, didn't see the Yankee regulars as "instructors" but as players who had jumped the March 1 training getaway, and chased all of us out of the desert after two weeks of it. I wouldn't know about that since I picked up some valuable tips from the established big leaguers before getting orders to beat it.

But what a two weeks before I headed back for Commerce. I mean my first close-up or close-listen-to and -of

Stengel. Casey greeted us with a speech, my introduction to that dog Latin I'd been hearing about. All I learned from his first oration is that "you fellers all have got a chance if you learn something about base runnin'."

During the first three days of the usual fundamentals, all I got from Stengel was an occasional wink. I could have been wrong, though. Because a fellow tenderfoot, George Prigge, a shortstop from Norfolk, believed I was muscling in on a flock of Casey's winks that were intended for him.

It wasn't until I had won a race held among the farm boys that Stengel honored me with his first personal conversation.

9

It's a Double–Negative

A Phoenix newspaperman prepared me for my first talk with Stengel. He warned me not only to listen but please to look because Casey "said" more with a twitch and a jerk than he did with a pair of ain'ts—back-to-back.

I thanked him and put up my guard. Ole Case broke through with the first gesture.

"You just keep chasing those jack rabbits," started Stengel, "and you'll get somewhere. . . . If it's one thing the Yankees can use it's more and better base runners. . . . Ain't no good ones around, anymore . . . you take a game we lost to Rolfe's [Red Rolfe, then manager of the Detroit Tigers] team. . . . If a certain feller had run to third . . . the Crow [Frank Crosetti] begged him to run . . . why we'da won the game and that would have made it a lot easier to win the pennant . . . I know we didn't win the pennant until the last day of the season but if we had beaten Rolfe's team the day I'm talkin' about, I'd have had my fresh pitchers for the other team and I could have changed my line-up and it would have been a lot easier . . . Son, if you ever learn how to bunt from either side with that speed, you ought to hit .400."

By that time Casey had danced a jig, curved his eyebrows behind his ears, threw his nose out of joint, and wound up with his favorite expression of surprise to the tune of those gosh-awful gasps of his. He went on, I kept listening—and looking.

"I like young fellers, like to play 'em in the big leagues when they're supposed to be too young to play in the big leagues. Now you go back out there on the field and keep practicin' what they're teaching you."

I practiced and learned. That's one of the Yankee secrets. They've got the coaches who can teach their know-how. Following my last intra-squad game, I received what I considered terrific news. They told me to go back home and await transportation to Lake Wales, Florida, where I was to train with the Kansas City club.

I felt so good I telephoned Commerce and told the folks all about it. I realized I was going to Florida only for the ride (and more instruction) but it made me feel—well, like a Yankee. A little one, anyway, because Dad told me over the phone it was a promotion.

The promotion carried me from Class D to Class C—to Joplin in the Western Association. To me, it was perfect for two reasons. Joplin was just across the Oklahoma line in Missouri and, more important, Harry Craft, my manager at Independence, had moved along with me.

While Harry didn't play any favorites, he seemed to give me extra attention. I thought so, anyway. And my baseball education continued. At the same time I kept striking out. It got so bad, at one point, I started to show my disgust by throwing the bat away. Craft soon broke me of that bad habit by threatening to bench me. It worked.

At Joplin, I could almost feel myself growing. By the middle of the season (in my eighteenth year) my weight jumped to 180 and I stood about five-eleven, my present height. I was beginning to get some distance.

When the season ended, I had 26 homers, 14 right-handed and 12 left-handed, 12 triples, and 30 doubles. Batted in 136 runs and hit .383 in 137 games—199 hits in 519 times at bat. I mention the .383 because I believe I won't ever hit that much again. Of course, I'll be trying. What ball-player doesn't?

But the .383 didn't help me as a fielder. The sports writers kept calling me an "erratic" shortstop. They really had something there. I had committed 55 errors. So in calling me "erratic," I guess they were nice. I had a hunch I wasn't as good as Phil Rizzuto, at that.

A couple of weeks later, I watched Rizzuto in action, as a guest of the Yankees. With the play-offs all over in the Western, I joined the Yankees in St. Louis in September, 1950. Furthermore, they told me I could hit with the team in the practices before the game. All I needed, naturally, was the invitation.

Harry Craft gave me the best advice yet, before I headed for St. Louis. After loading me up with all kinds of encouragement about going places in the game, Harry said, "You're going to make a lot of new and influential friends as you advance in baseball but remember this—don't forget your old ones. They're the ones who made you."

On my way to St. Louis, I was happier than a barefoot boy who had shot his first quail. But when I got there, I would have run all the way back home if anyone had hollered "Git!" in the lobby of the Chase Hotel.

Those Yankees operated too fast for me. Frankly, the manner in which they mobbed in there, bag and baggage, gave me the jitters. Pretty soon, everybody was being paged from Red Patterson (public relations chief) to Whitey Ford. And to make matters worse, Patterson seemed to be arguing with four or five sports writers (they weren't built like ballplayers, anyway) about some story that "broke" in a place where it wasn't supposed to or something like that. I still don't know how they "break" them.

Then it got crazier because fifteen minutes later Patterson was eating breakfast at the same table with about eight of those writing fellows. And here's the catch. Everybody was laughing, including Red.

I only managed to get up a sweat in St. Louis because I was too afraid or too bashful to enter the batting cage. But I was right on that hunch about not being another Rizzuto. Phil showed me enough in the infield drills to give me an idea that I'd better make it at some other position. Dad already had discussed my chances as an outfielder with Harry Craft some weeks before but I didn't know it.

By the time we (the Yankees) hit Chicago, I felt a little more at home. What made it easier was that I had a new partner in crime. They had just signed a former star football player from Purdue—Bill Skowron. So Bill, a powerfully built guy, and I muscled in and hit a few before the regulars took over. I liked Skowron. Turned out to be the same slugger who hit .341 at Kansas City in 1952.

The honeymoon (steak three times a day if you wanted it and the plushiest kind of train and hotel accommodations) soon ended just before the Yankees headed for New York and another World Series. While telling me good-by, Stengel said he'd be seeing me at the Phoenix school again in February, 1951. I told him I could stand a little more schooling and returned to Commerce to pass the winter and await instructions.

Came the following February and I waited and waited and waited. No letters and no instructions. They had forgotten me. That was it. Oh, well, what could a Class C Leaguer expect. Finally, while working at Blue Goose No. 1 and getting more worried by the day, I received a long-distance call from Phoenix. They wanted to know why in the thunderation I hadn't shown up with the rest of the fellows.

Bursting with excitement but playing hard to get, I calmly replied, "I'm broke and have no money for transportation." Somebody cussed loudly before the operator cut us óff. A couple of hours later the local telegraph office called me. There were money and instructions as to what train to catch. I caught it in plenty of time. My bag had been packed since October.

10

Ben Epstein: Background

Oasis in the Desert

Del E. Webb, a big league contractor of Phoenix, realized the second of his two sports dreams in the spring of 1951. Webb accomplished the first one when he along with Daniel R. Topping, the tin plate heir, and promotional genius Leland Stanford (Larry) MacPhail, engineered the purchase of the Yankee empire from the estate of Colonel Jacob Ruppert for the reported unbelievable bargain of $2,-800,000 in February, 1945.

Webb's second ambition as a sportsman was to show the Yankees before his Arizona home folks. After all, the Bombers represented the class of baseball. Since Del assumed the role of a co-owner, the Yanks scored under the management of Bucky Harris in 1947 and by the shots of Casey Stengel in 1949 and 1950. Then, as now, the stadium in the Bronx ruled the roost as the home of champions.

Indeed, transferring the Bombers from their established spring training base in St. Petersburg, to the Phoenix sands

47

had churned through Del's head since 1946 when the government lifted the travel bans following World War II. However, it was out of the question at the time. As a vice-president and general manager, MacPhail already had contracted for pre-St. Petersburg siestas in Panama and Puerto Rico in 1946 and 1947 and maybe Madagascar in the future. But Larry resigned during an emotional fit on the last day of the 1947 series between the Yankees and the Dodgers, and retired to his horses and cows at his Maryland Shangri-La.

With the exodus of MacPhail, the Yankees resumed their conservative system of operation as under the direction of Edward Grant Barrow, Ruppert's guiding hand, and currently George M. Weiss, whose administrative intelligence in running the vast organization is second to none.

It is understood that Webb discussed his "civic pride" venture with Topping and Weiss as early as 1948. The rub, of course, stemmed from the fact that Phoenix played spring-training host to a very welcome client—the New York Giants. Moreover, the St. Pete sponsors didn't enjoy the prospect of losing the Yanks (the top March attraction for its thousands of winter visitors) for a day—much less a season.

Webb, however, finally swung the deal after considerable placating and assorted legalistics and promises. The Yankee brass had managed to swap training sites with the Giants for 1951. Webb, thanks to the cooperation of Horace Stoneham, Giant president, put it over. "His" Yankees were coming to Phoenix for exercises and exhibitions in addition to an extensive tour of the Pacific Coast. Previously, the Yanks hadn't trained farther West than New Orleans.

By the time Stengel concluded his second school during

the last week in February, a majority of the men listed on the Yankee roster for 1951 had reported, awaiting March 1, official training getaway. The fans, Yankee-hungry, came to see Di Maggio, Rizzuto, Berra, Reynolds, Raschi, Lopat, Woodling, Mize (remembered as an old Giant hand), Bauer, and others.

Sands Begin to Stir

Needless to say, the Yankees appeared equally impressive in the Mountain Time Zone as they did in the Eastern and Standard belts. Preliminary workouts are the same everywhere, but there's an intangible air about the pitch-and-catch and Pepper games of the Bombers which give them a ring of authority—the dividend of being a champ.

All that, plus the pantomime of Stengel, balances the program, as it were. Yet, it must be remembered Casey's clowning is partly extra-curricular and partly psychological. Actually, Stengel's antics, which also include temperamental spasms, conceal an artist who must be ranked as one of baseball's all-time managers. Tactically, his knowledge of strategy and the handling of men may rank him above his illustrious Yankee predecessors, Miller Huggins and Joe McCarthy.

Coloring (or clouding up) this 1951 Arizona backdrop stand the gentlemen of the metropolitan press. Those in attendance at Phoenix to report Casey's charting of his third pennant in the desert country and draw their daily ration of yuks, included Daniel M. Daniel, *World-Telegram and Sun* and *The Sporting News;* James P. Dawson, *Times;* Joseph Trimble, *Daily News;* Hugh Bradley, *Journal-American;* Harold Rosenthal, *Herald Tribune;* Arch Murray, *Post;*

Hy Goldberg, Newark *Evening News;* Gayle Talbot, *Associated Press;* Jack Orr, *Compass;* and me, *Daily Mirror.*

Something buzzed in the ether or, as Stengel defines the higher altitudes, "the stratmosphere." You could feel it. The camp jumped with stories, and the subject or subjects stalked among the minor leaguers, the Bombers' blood bank. It was harvest time for the Yankees, although none suspected, not even planter-in-chief George Weiss, the class of the crop.

The writers didn't need an interpreter following a week of drills and an all-farm roster game with Cleveland, the Indian greenies bussing over from Tuscon. Stengel, in his "reconstruction job" and accent on youth, admitted he had been sold on the very same kids whom the scribes began to mention and then play up in their daily files: Gil McDougald, Tom Morgan, and Mickey Mantle.

"We've decided to keep those three around a little longer," said Casey, following wholesale discharges to make room for the regulars. He read from the back of an envelope. "McDougald is a second baseman who I'm gonna try at third. Morgan handles himself pretty well and Turner tells me his control is good as anybody's on the club. He's from Binghamton.

"Mantle is a shortstop up from Joplin on the Binghamton roster for 1951. He's a shortstop and he ain't much of a shortstop, either. But he sure can switch-hit hard, and run as fast as anybody I ever saw. I've seen some pretty good runners and ole Case was a pretty fair runner, himself. You fellers be out here tomorrow and you might see this Mantle at a place that could surprise you."

The "fellers" were out bright and early the next morning. And they spotted the "surprise" in nothing flat. Tommy

Henrich, now a coach, was talking to Mantle. He led Mickey into the outfield, had another huddle, left him there, and started fun-going fly balls to him. Nothing sensational there. Then they played an intra-camp game and Mantle lined up in *center field* for the Yannigans. It was the first time he ever had played in the outfield, anyplace, anywhere.

Batting left-handed against the right-handed Wally Hood, Mickey slugged a one-run triple in the first inning and two-run out-of-the-park homer in the second. He made only one put-out during the nine innings but the writers had observed the Yankee trade-mark—power. So, in a body, they wired their respective desks the crazy prediction: that *"In Mickey Mantle, the Yankees are grooming the successor to Joe Di Maggio!"*

Going Mad About Mickey

Mantle's center field "experience" embraced only six more innings in another intra-camper before the Yankees opened the 1951 exhibition season against the Indians at Tucson on March 10. The game attracted 5,380, a new crowd record, and the fans received their money's worth in the fourth inning. Stengel, for the fans' sake, let Di Maggio hit for Bob Porterfield.

The Bombers lost, 6–5, but Casey disdained suicide and you can guess why. Mickey, going all the way in his first competition against big leaguers, led the twelve-hit attack with three—two singles and a double. More important, he smacked those two singles off a pretty fair country pitcher, Early Wynn. We journalists went daffy.

Those three rookies looked as if they all had a chance to wind up on triple-A teams before the club broke camp. Besides Mantle, McDougald, operating at third for the first time, flashed the poise of a veteran; and Morgan held the Tribe to one hit, fanned one, and walked none in three innings. Not bad at all when you realize that Tom threw against such people as Larry Doby, Dale Mitchell, Al Rosen, Minny Minoso, Bobby Avila, Harry Simpson, and Ray Boone.

Cleveland returned the compliment the following day in the Phoenix opener before 7,398. For turnstile reasons, Mantle was limited to two innings in this one, won by the Yankees, 13–8. Di Maggio hit a pinch-hit homer, Mize socked a three-runner, and, to keep the rookies in the running, Clint Courtney, a bespectacled catcher, now with the Browns, hit a three-run homer and a one-run double.

Then, as they say, they couldn't get Mickey out. He continued socking away in a blazing streak unparalleled in the history of a Yankee training camp. It was the same on the Coast; at Hollywood, Los Angeles, Glendale (Stengel's home town), Sacramento, San Francisco, Oakland, and back to Los Angeles against the University of Southern California.

It was on the Southern Cal campus that he experienced his first case of being an "idol." For on that afternoon, the Yankees' sixteenth exhibition to date, Mantle whammed two tremendous two-run homers, a two-run triple, and a single for good measure. Mickey needed the protection of a strong-arm squad to squeeze into the Yankee bus. The enthusiastic students fought for the autograph of a nineteen-year-old kid who was younger than most of them.

I recall a remark Gene Markland made to me during this push: "I've seen many a phenom in my day but this Mantle is the phenominginest phenom I ever saw."

It seemed a natural observation and Markland wasn't the first. Branch Rickey dropped in for a gander at Los Angeles. After Mickey blasted a 450-footer before the Deacon's saucered eyes, he ushered a note to Topping, seated in an adjoining box, "Would be most interested if you care to deal him."

Earlier a fascinated Frank Lane, general manager of the White Sox, spieled, "I'll give the Yankees a quarter of a million for him and bury him in $1,000 bills as a bonus."

Lane couldn't have gotten him for Fort Knox, without tax. The Yankees started stepping up Mantle's pace, an obvious acceleration, one thought, after Di Maggio hinted he would hang them up after 1951.

How About That?

By the time the Yankees returned to Phoenix to open a series with Paul Richards' White Sox on March 27, Mantle was the most publicized baseball player in the country. Small wonder, as headlines began praising the Oklahoma teenager as "The Sweet Switcher, Commerce Comet, Oakie Doakie," etc.

Mickey, of course, boomed on . . . against the White Sox, Pirates, and the Indians again. Before the Bombers headed East, Red Patterson compiled Mantle's average for twenty-four games. Mel Allen was delineating the scenic wonders of Arizona as viewed from the rooftop of a grandstand when Patterson handed him the statistics on Mickey. With that, Allen abruptly left a kaleidoscopic shadow dangling on Camel Back Mountain and screamed to his New York listeners, "Mantle is hitting .431! How about that?"

Mel, a Yankee fan, had yelped "How about that's?" before and he'll do it in the future, but Allen's outburst on this particular occasion definitely stands out as his most sten- torian and hysterical "How about that?" on record.

Meanwhile, the "boss" had returned to center field. And with Di Maggio in the middle again, Mantle alternated in left and right (where a fly ball once bounced off his head) and never stopped collecting from one to four hits per game.

Mickey had just socked the sixth Yankee homer in the sixth inning of a game played in a sandstorm at El Paso (there were 6,473 in the house) when my operator tapped out a message.

"Wire story out of Tulsa," it read, "says Mantle called for second army physical. What about it? Please rush and don't forget to remember it's two hours later from where I sit. "It was signed by Jack Hennigan of the *Mirror* sports desk.

At the same time Dawson of the *Times*, Trimble of the *News*, and Rosenthal of the *Herald Tribune* had received similar inquiries. Daniel of the *World Telly* already had been tipped off by the UP and passed it along to Bradley, Mur- ray, Orr, and Goldberg. They braved the storm in search of Patterson, who was conspicuously absent, always a sure sign that something brewed.

The afternoon papers crew corralled Red and backed him into the press box where he corroborated the report. Pat- terson confessed he didn't know exactly why, since he al- ready had been declared 4-F in December, 1950.

The "why" however, was soon exposed. Washington, Gen- eral Lewis Hershey, Director of Selective Service, to be exact, had been receiving letters and had passed them on to Mantle's State Board.

It all stemmed, of course, from the coast-to-coast publicity. The text of most of the mail wanted to know how a 4-F could hit a baseball so far and run so fast.

Daniel's Big Scoop

On the long haul from El Paso to San Antonio, Mickey officially learned that his second examination was still a week away and decided to ride along until the club hit Kansas City, and from there his father would take him to Tulsa.

The added pressure didn't seem to bother Mantle one whit as the Yanks rolled through Austin, Beaumont, Houston, and against the Braves at Dallas and Kansas City. It was in the latter city that Daniel shared a big scoop with his fellow scribes.

Mickey already had headed for Tulsa, via his Commerce home, when Dan sent out his trial balloon. The scene, a hotel room where all the boys assembled for quick showers and shaves. He picked up a phone, called the Kansas City Draft Board, and asked the status of osteomyelitis cases relative to exemption from the draft.

Speaking to the draft board physician, Dan was informed the disease carried automatic disqualification. This has since been superseded by a ruling that one is qualified for the service if osteomyelitis is successfully treated for two or more years.

While gaining this valuable information (certainly to the New York press) Dan merely acknowledged receipt of same with his characteristic "yeah, yeah, yeah," and "yeah." He thanked the officer, cradled the receiver, and turned to his anxious confederates.

"Well?" asked Rosenthal as a feeler to break the tension.

No answer. Dan buttoned his vest.

"Benny and I have a deadline to make," snapped Trimble, "what did he say?"

No answer. Dan adjusted his tie and cleared his throat.

"Hurry up, will you?" demanded Dawson, "I want to get some lunch."

No answer. Dan started to swell in his characteristic pomposity.

Bradley used diplomacy. "Save it for the afternoon papers."

Hugh's proposition to form an entente snapped Dan out of his trance. Dan is a well-preserved man for his years and often is referred to as the Daniel Webster of Rockville Centre, Long Island, particularly when he rises to address his or anybody else's constituents. Too, Dan has a driving voice, two octaves above a threshing machine, which on clear days can be heard in center field. He slowly expanded himself to full stature and began.

"Gentlemen!" He drove the word through the wall, then rasped on. *"The man (Mantle) is rejected. You can write it."*

We wrote it. Dan was right. That the man was rejected was confirmed two days later by the Oklahoma Draft Board.

On the eve of the annual interborough spring series between the Yankees and the Dodgers, Mickey boarded a plane at Tulsa and flew all night to show up at Ebbets Field in time for his metropolitan début.

He got four hits including a homer. The big day enabled nineteen-year-old Mickey Mantle to hit a sensational .402 for the spring exhibitions of 1951. His 41–for–102 included seven doubles, a triple, and nine homers. He had batted in thirty-one runs.

A new star had been born.

11

Just Plumb Scared

Brooklyn is wonderful even if it hasn't got any fish hatcheries in Prospect Park, but I wouldn't advise any nineteen-year-old country boy to play his first New York baseball in Ebbets Field. That is, if he can't help it and I couldn't help it in April, 1951, after I flew all night to get to the place.

Stengel noticed I looked sort of peaked. He thought I was tired from my long airplane ride, and asked me if I wanted another day off to get my bearings straight. When I told him I felt O.K., he looked at the stands and actually chuckled.

"Fans over here might seem a little different to you," he said, "but they won't bite you. Played the outfield over here as early as 1912 and they liked me so well they didn't fire me until 1917. Then they brought me back as a manager in 1934 and fired me again at the end of 1936. But they were so crazy about me they paid me just for doing nothing in 1937."

Stengel's talking also eased me somewhat. He also explained that all those sports writers on field didn't mean any harm. I never did quite get it when he told me all they wanted was a story of some kind since that's the way they made a living. He also cackled something about not paying any attention to what the fans shouted.

To tell you the truth, that's what bothered me. For after I got my first hit, some fellow popped up and screamed, "Who do you think you are—Musial? Ya bum!"

Somebody told me, I forget who it was, that the fans would be a lot nicer in the Bronx. I didn't doubt it, but not when they're playing the Dodgers. Because I swear I heard that same fellow holler at me from the right-field stands in the Yankee Stadium, "I still say you can't carry Musial's glove, ya bum!" I wanted to break his neck even though I had to agree with him.

I'd be lying if I denied reading the New York papers—all of them. And I must admit I noticed all the sports pages had me starting the 1951 season for the Yankees in right field. What puzzled me was that I didn't know—one way or the other. That's what made it so embarrassing. Sports writers were asking me how it felt before I ever played it.

I never knew for sure until the night before we were scheduled to open in Washington. The team just had pulled out of Pennsylvania Station when Stengel called me into his compartment. It was after that huddle I learned that he had separate sets of languages. One for the press and another for the players.

"I'm going to see how you look in right field tomorrow," Stengel started. He was all business. "Don't try to be what they [the writers] say you are, because you can't be that good. Just don't be afraid, and hustle. That's one thing I'm sure about, your hustle. Now go back to your seat and relax. We'll be in Washington in a few hours."

I thanked him and left and sat down and shook. I never stopped shaking all night, even in the swanky Shoreham Hotel. I wished for Harry Craft, who managed me at Independence and Joplin. He had been sent to manage Beaumonth which, to me, seemed to fit my breeches. As I said earlier, that's the way Dad and I had planned it. And this seemed way over my head.

The game at Washington was postponed because of rain and the team returned to New York. I was glad and then got scared all over again when I suddenly realized we were going to play the first of two with the Red Sox in the stadium the very next day.

No help. It didn't rain. And, sure enough, there was my name, as big as you please, on the line-up pasted up in the dugout. I batted third behind Rizzuto with Jensen leading off. Di Maggio hit clean-up and was followed by Berra, Mize, Billy Johnson, and Jerry Coleman. Raschi pitched.

I'll always remember that line-up because it was my big league first. Never thought I could make it to right field but something Berra said got the blood moving again in my legs. Yogi wasn't talking to anybody in particular. But I knew it would take more than a ball game, World Series or rounders, to addle Mr. Berra.

"What kind of opening is this?" beefed Yogi. "Ain't no people here!"

To me that sounded like a crazy remark because I saw a lot of people; more than I had ever seen in one spot. Of course, the stadium is a pretty big spot. There were about 45,000 of them, and that's about twenty times the population of Commerce—a crowd apt to make a rookie going out for the first time a little bit on the tense side.

Bill Wight started for the Red Sox; and the funny thing

about it was that I wasn't worried so much about Wight, a good left-hand pitcher with that gosh-awful move to first base, as I was about Boston's left-fielder.

Ted Williams made me nervous. I just happened to remember that Williams was one of the greatest left-hand distance and pull hitters of all time, and that I was in right field and didn't even know how to adjust my sun glasses. After all, it was only a few weeks earlier, in a Phoenix intra-camper, that a fly ball bounced off my head because I couldn't properly flip the specs.

Since Lou Boudreau wasn't available, Cliff Mapes told me how to play Ted. "Just back up as far as you can," said Mapes, "and set yourself for line drives, sinkers, sailers, and, oh, yes—homers." I was sorry Cliff gave me that information because it scared me all the more.

Luckily for me, Williams singled to center, flied to left (Ted must have been in the mood), then walked and forced a runner in three trips. Walt Dropo flied to me for the first out in the second inning for my first big league put-out. Coleman cheered me up with an "attaboy" and I settled down, if you can call my knees knocking every two seconds instead of one settling down.

I wound up with three put-outs. Caught a Vern Stephens fly in the fourth and Bobby Doerr hit me one in the ninth. By that time Raschi was coasting, shutting out the Red Sox, 5–0, with a six-hitter. All he needed was Jensen's two-run homer in the third.

I must tell you about my first big league hit. It was a long time coming. I thought so, anyway. Bobby Doerr threw me out in the first after I broke my bat. I popped out to Stephens in the third but hit pay dirt (it was to me) in the sixth.

Jensen, still hot, opened the inning with a double and Jackie took third after Rizzuto was safe on a sacrifice and fielder's choice. Batting right-handed against Wight, I singled between short and third to score Jensen and became a happy man for at least a day.

I even was happier the next day when I got a two-run single, right-handed, off Harry Taylor in a four-run fifth inning. Lopat heroed in spades. Not only did he pitch a two-hitter and a no-hitter for six for a 6–3 win, but Ed hit a two-run homer off Ellis Kinder in the eighth.

Then I began to learn the facts of big league life. The Yankees could also lose, and that we did in our first game at Washington. Worse still, I showed up with my number one weakness—striking out. Sandy Consuegra fanned me twice and that only was the beginning.

I had averaged a strike-out per game during the first five and began to press. I also was aware of the fact that the American League pitching had an edge on the kind I had been seeing at Joplin. I got lucky in our first against the Athletics and got three for five against Lou Brissie and Hank Wyse. My average jumped to .320.

By this time I started to get chummy with the boys as we prepared for our first Western trip. Frankly, I yearned to get in on those hearts games generally played in the Yankees' special diner (this is the year before the Twenty Questions incident) after all the steaks were cleaned out.

I played (and beat) some of the boys at snooker during the spring training days, so I figured maybe I'd try my luck at cards. The games really would get exciting—especially the hearts battles among Reynolds, Lopat, Joe Collins, and Ralph Houk with Raschi serving as the chief sweater. "Sweater," I learned, is a guy who second-guesses the players and explains why they lost.

The number two game always involved Rizzuto and anybody he could round up. During my first Western trip, I noticed Phil had trouble whipping up a foursome. So I politely asked Rizzuto if he could use me in an emergency. Phil, always kidding, cut me down to his size—but fast.

"I like your nerve," screamed Phil, drawing himself up to his full five-feet-six. "The idea of a busher like you asking to play with me. Son, you've got a lot to learn. Come back in a couple of years and I might consider letting you sit next to me. Besides, you're still a minor."

Rizzuto then dealt me a hand. You have to love him. But Phil still gets sick when he tries to smoke a cigar. Me, too.

I dropped to .222 before I hit my first big league homer. It was in Chicago on May 1, off Randy Gumpert. And it was a pretty good one—might have been one of my longest. The ball reached the extreme end of the right-field stands. The paper said it traveled about 450 feet.

I ran into my first "trouble" with Red Patterson in Chicago on this particular trip. I forgot to pack my bag and leave it in the hotel lobby for collection on getaway day. So when I found myself heading for the depot and St. Louis, I told Red about my suitcase.

Patterson hit the roof. But he delivered. Red grabbed a cab, rushed out to the Hotel Del Prado, Yankee headquarters there. The cab waited while he poured everything he could find into my bag, and beat it back to the depot. Patterson arrived a minute before the train pulled out. He forgave me after warning me never to let that happen again. Red also swore he crammed those two Del Prado towels into my bag by mistake.

I still was striking out. Stengel, however, continued to go along with me, although he didn't like the idea of risking me for a full nine innings as a fielder in winning ball games. Meanwhile, Casey worked on my throwing, and had me lifting my leg like a pitcher. An Oklahoma friend of mine and an old Giant fan who saw me in St. Louis said I tried to throw like Mel Ott used to hit.

I managed to hang above .300 until late May. But I kept striking out and my average began to sink. Then I died in Boston in a double-header on May 30. Before Stengel jerked me out, in the seventh inning of the opener (the Sox won, 11–10 in fifteen) I went down swinging three straight times to Chuck Stobbs. Casey gave me a second chance in the second game and after Will Nixon fanned me twice (that's five in a row), I cried like a baby.

I bawled to Stengel, "Put somebody in there who can hit the ball. I can't."

Stengel understood. Mapes finished the game in right. We lost a double-header.

12

Down and Almost Out

I felt ashamed and a little silly after my crying jag in Boston. Stengel let me get it out of my system before he told me he was starting me in the next series in Detroit. His decision reminded me of a story I had heard about Joe McCarthy from either Dickey or Crosetti. That is, McCarthy would never sour on a player who gave his best, no matter what the fans or the critics thought of him.

Even so, I saw it coming. The end, I mean. Casey let me have it in easy stages. After being relieved by Jensen in the ninth of a twelve-inning game broken up by Berra's homer in the twelfth (how that Yogi can connect in Briggs Stadium) I went 0–for–5 in the first of a double-header against Bob Feller at Cleveland before 75,000 the next day. Feller won, 8–3.

I watched the second from the bench and wished I was back in the mines. Bob Lemon beat us, 4–1.

No use for me to look at the line-up, any more. I had been reduced to a no- or part-time player. Being a .261 hitter, I agreed. I was back in right during the next series in St.

64

Louis, and I'll always believe Stengel did it out of considera-
tion for my folks who had come up from Commerce for the
games. Casey is like that, but he protected himself in the
best possible way by batting me seventh.

I hung around for the rest of the Western trip and during
the following home stand, when I managed to connect about
once in every other town, which is about the best reason I
know why I couldn't climb out of the .260 bracket. We were
back in Cleveland on July 12, and my transfer to the taller
corn stood out like Gene Woodling's muscles.

But I was rewarded with an unforgettable going-away
gift although my leaving wasn't completely official at the
time. That night Allie Reynolds pitched a no-hitter to beat
Bob Feller, 1–0, on Woodling's homer in the seventh. Gene
is just as tough in Cleveland as Berra is in Detroit.

I was proud of the Chief and not because he comes
from Oklahoma, either. Allie really "mowed 'em down" with
his quick stuff. And when he's quick, he's quick, especially
under the lights. Ask anybody, even a Dodger, but Reynolds
is the kind of pitcher who can keep a batter honest.

That's the evening the Yanks (all but the Chief) got their
big scare. For after Allie fanned Feller (who only threw a
four-hitter) and knocked off Dale Mitchell on a fly and
Bobby Avila on a foul to finish the bottom of the sixth inning, he inched over to Berra and said, "I believe I can pitch
a no-hitter." Yogi passed out and everybody died because
it still was 0–0 at the time. You just don't say these things
during such goings-on. But what are you going to do when
the pitcher quits his own religion in a spot like this?

Personally, I didn't believe Allie got it until he made
Mitchell ground out for the second out in the ninth. To me,

Dale is the most dangerous hitter I know. He's from Oklahoma, too.

The next day (it would be July 13) I wrote my own ticket back to the minors.

Lemon struck me out three times as lead-off hitter in a knock-down drag-out won by the Indians, 11–8. What made it worse is that we led, 4–0, after three. That dropped the Yanks two and a half games into second place, and the surprising White Sox had taken charge during the first half of the season.

It also upped my strike-outs to 52 in 246 times at bat. That was enough for Stengel. He called me up to his room the next morning. Casey acted as it were a routine job, but I could see the Yankee farm system lit up in both eyes. And I was so disgusted with myself I didn't care much one way or the other.

"Mickey," Stengel said and I could see he was sorry, "you're getting a little nervous and tight at the plate . . . swinging at too many bad pitches. You're gonna develop into a big league star one of these days . . . that's my opinion, anyway. But, maybe a change of scenery might do you a lot of good. I'm going to send you to Kansas City as soon as we reach Detroit and you're going to play center field there."

He then tried to console me about my leading the club in runs-batted-in and that I had a chance to go places and some other white lies. I returned to my room and stayed there. I might have jumped out of the Cleveland hotel window if Casey hadn't mentioned center field. That's the job I wanted.

Red Patterson escorted me to the airport in Detroit. He had a ticket (one-way to Milwaukee where Kansas City was playing a series). Red noticed something wet about both of my eyes and said, "You'll be back to play in the next World Series." Patterson was nice and it helped ease a lot of the pain.

I reported to Selkirk (George "Twinkle Toes" Selkirk, Blues' manager and former Yankee outfielder famous as Ruth's right-field replacement) and—well, he knew the score. George told me he was glad to see me, that the Blues could stand a little, etc. If Selkirk had known how down I was, he'd have used a needle.

George almost went out of his mind, I guess, while he wondered when and if I could help him. I beat out a bunt in my first time up in my new uniform and then went 0-for-19. That was my "average" when we returned to Kansas City. I had given up. I felt as if I couldn't make the grade again at Independence.

Dad showed up at Kansas City. I gave it to him straight, telling how I had folded and couldn't stop. I ended it all by hinting that I wasn't cut out for baseball and that I had let him down, much as I hated to say it and wanted to spare his feelings.

Dad didn't say a word. He just let me rave and rave. The cork finally exploded and I wound up bawling. Dad knew a lot more about my bawling and I got no sympathy. He gave it to me, man-to-man. I say that because he had never talked to me that way before.

"Mickey," he said quietly, "you can't have it easy all your life. Baseball is no different from any other job. Things get tough once in a while and you must learn how to take it— the sooner the better. It takes guts, not moaning, to make it. And if that's all the guts you have, I agree with you. You don't belong in baseball. Come on back to Commerce and grub out a living in the mines for the rest of your life."

Dad ended up by saying he'd be seeing me at the ball park or mines, and left. He looked bad. A husky 190-pounder, Dad had lost about twenty pounds. He complained about a "misery" in his back that kept getting "worse all the time."

Deep down, I knew my failure pained him more than that ache in his back. So I decided to give it another whirl. Dad saw me again—at the ball park.

I suffered from a ball-player's common ailment; and Rizzuto says there's nothing wrong with a player that a base hit can't cure. There's a lot to what he says. Once I got the "cure" at Kansas City, I remembered I had been farmed to the Blues subject to twenty-four-hour recall, and I was determined to be recalled.

But there was only one way to get back. And that was to deliver in the American Association. Once you swing through it—Milwaukee, Minneapolis, Louisville, Indianapolis, Toledo, St. Paul, and K.C.—you not only play in some classy ball parks but run into a lot of capable managers.

During my short stay with the Blues, I watched such guys running the show as Charley Grimm, Clay Hopper, Pinky Higgins, Tommy Heath, Jack Tighe, Don Gutteridge, and Harry Walker. I kept right on learning. And Selkirk didn't hurt me any, either. George at times reminded me of Tommy Henrich, and that was good enough for me.

After forty games in the A.A., I was hitting .361, exactly 101 points better than my Yankee average I left in Detroit earlier in the season. Got sixty hits in 166 times at bat for 108 total bases including nine doubles, three triples, and eleven homers, and I batted in fifty runs.

During August I received that recall, with instructions to

join the Yankees at Cleveland (seems like it's always Cleveland) on the twenty-fourth of the month. When I arrived there that morning, the Yankees were in second place—three games behind the Indians. The White Sox, by this time, had faded out of the race, being in fourth place and thirteen games off the pace.

Stengel greeted me with a wink and seemed glad to see me. He mumbled something about my Kansas City .381 being safe for the time-being, because Lemon had beaten Raschi and the Yankees the day before, 2–1, with a three-hitter.

Casey then asked if I was ready and I said I was. So I returned to right field. Stubby Overmire and Joe Ostrowski surprised everybody by shutting out the Indians, 2–0, on Woodling's two-run homer off Early Wynn in the seventh.

That chopped Cleveland's lead to two games. The next day we squeezed the difference to one. We beat Mike Garcia, 7–3, and I am sticking out my chest for a minute: I hit a two-run homer in the third. I'm boasting because Garcia is the toughest pitcher I ever faced, and still is.

The chances are I'd change my mind about Garcia if I faced Reynolds or Raschi on one of their good days (which I hope is never) but, as of now, I've got to give it to Mike. He just blazes them at me in spots I don't like too well. I can't tell you exactly where, but they must be somewhere in the strike zone—all the umps seem to agree.

We moved on to Chicago where we split a pair with the White Sox, who still were running even though they were out of it by now. We then beat the Browns twice in St. Louis, the second win, 15–2, putting us in a tie with the Indians for the league lead on August 29.

I played right field and the folks were up and I was happy.

I singled and homered and batted in four runs. The game reminded me of a game played on the previous May 3 in St. Louis when we beat the Browns, 17–3, and scored eleven runs in the ninth inning. Gil McDougald and Jackie Jensen went crazy in that inning. Each hit a triple and a homer and Gil's two hits batted in six runs which, I believe, tie a record. Jackie's hits batted in only two. Fact is, Jensen also doubled in the third for only three RBI's for the day. It's all in the situation, I guess.

After another dip into second place, we took the top on September 16 and held it the rest of the way. Cleveland came to town in first place by a game. This was it. Reynolds beat Feller, 5–1, with a five-hitter before 68,000 in the opener. And in the most thrilling play I ever saw, we won the second, 2–1, in the ninth for Lopat when Rizzuto bunted off Lemon to squeeze Di Maggio home. I had the best seat in the stadium, being in the batter's slot at the time. But I wasn't on my knees.

13

Buckled and Bowed

I was dreaming of fried catfish dancing on toasted biscuits the morning of September 28, 1951, when the eight o'clock "alarm clock" went off. The "clock" in the form of bath towels pinged me on the head, on the feet and in the middle, and mostly in the middle when I slept on my stomach.

The stinging end of the towels were snapped by my gentle roommates, Johnny Hopp and Hank Bauer. The three of us shared a midtown Manhattan apartment when the Yanks were at home. Under the agreement, Hopp cooked, Bauer cleaned up, and I was the errand boy and can-opener-in-chief. It's the price of being a rookie.

"All right, dreamboat," cracked Johnny between his stingers, "it's time to grab your gun and go to the store and rustle up some coffee, us menfolk are hungry and thirsty." Hank just laughed and threw a glass of water in my face to make sure I'd heard. Those Marines can't help but play rough, even in the morning.

"And another thing, sonny boy," added Hopp. "It might

be a good idea to show up at the stadium a little bit on the early side today. According to the paper, we can win a couple today and then start figuring out ways to spend some World Series money. That might wake you up."

I didn't need a shower to remind me that two wins on this particular day would clinch the third straight pennant for the Yankees. It was a Friday. We opened a double-header with the Red Sox, the beginning of a five-game series.

Since I had played the day before against the A's, I figured on maybe getting in on one of the two against Boston. What I forgot to consider, however, was that Bobby Shantz had beaten us, 4–1, with a six-hitter and Stengel seldom works the same combination after a loss. But don't ask me to explain it. All I know is that it works. I've heard players say Casey had his reasons, but I didn't think it wise for me to sound him out. Billy Martin would. In fact, Martin insisted that he hit fourth.

Stengel would pay Billy no mind, though. He acted as if he expected it and only seemed concerned about Martin when Billy wouldn't give him any back talk. I began to understand later when they paired Martin and me as roomies. Billy is just one stack of sass who can teach you plenty about inside baseball. He used to room with Cookie Lavagetto when he played with Oakland on the Coast.

Casey went with his best against the Red Sox. Reynolds had been named to pitch the opener and Raschi, the second. Above Reynolds in that first one was Rizzuto, Coleman, Bauer, Di Maggio, McDougald, Berra, Woodling, and Collins. Mize had been alerted to keep his muzzle-loader warm, just in case.

I was on the far end of the bench, next to the water cooler. But it was a ringside seat, a lookout from where I began to understand how and why the Yankees win the big ones. It was so wonderful I even forgot I had been "slighted" —but this wasn't for kids just back from Kansas City.

Then Reynolds pitched that no-hitter, his second of the year, against Mel Parnell to clinch a tie for the pennant. That's the one in which Berra muffed Ted Williams' last out 3–2 foul before he caught another Williams foul to end it.

I played right field in Allie's first no-hitter against the Indians and suffered a case of fidgets I thought I'd never duplicate. But, take it from me, those July fidgets were nothing compared to the September fidgets I got while watching on the bench.

Unlike the one in Cleveland, the Chief didn't floor Yogi by telling him he believed he could pitch a no-hitter with three innings to go. Reynolds didn't say anything to anybody. I had a hunch Allie was going to do it again as early as the second inning.

That's when he struck out Williams for the third out in the first and had Clyde Vollmer and Billy Goodman doing the same thing for the first two outs in the second. I recall Reynolds was standing at the plate when Berra made the muff and he just returned to the mound and made Ted do it again. I began to understand what they mean by "champion" who needed only the first of two runs in the first (straight singles by Rizzuto, Coleman, and Bauer) to do it. The score was 8–0.

I'll always remember Allie's comment after it was all over, "Well, it's nice to know I'm the first one to ever do it in the American League." Somebody kidded the Chief about not doing it the hard way like Johnny Vander Meer, who did it in succession for the Reds against the Braves and the

Dodgers in 1938. Reynolds said something about not wanting to be a hog about it and let it go at that.

Raschi breezed to the pennant in the second game as the Yankees knocked out Bill Wight in a seven-run second inning. Vic gave up six hits, three of them in the first when the Red Sox scored the first two of their three runs. Boston got its third run in the second on two wild pitches.

We broke loose in the bottom of the inning on Rizzuto's two-run single, Bauer's one-run single, and rolled the seven on McDougald's three-run triple. It was Gil's second time up in the inning. Di Maggio hit a three-run homer off Chuck Stobbs in the sixth. It didn't mean much at the time, but it turned out to be Joe's final homer of his career in regular season competition—No. 361.

I finished the series and the season in center field as the regulars rested and spent all their time working out and talking and reading about that Giant miracle. Seems that most of the older Yanks rooted for the Giants in that gaga play-off with the Dodgers. It was nothing personal but they all knew the Polo Grounds seated twice as many as Ebbets Field.

I didn't get it—at first. But I soon fell in line. I know it's commercial, but one is inclined to become cash-minded once you put on a Yankee uniform. Woodling simplified it for me. "The more pennants you win," he said, "the more money you make. That's why I'm here." And if that's bad . . . it isn't when you make it your profession.

The night I was reading all about Bobby Thomson's "impossible" pennant homer off Ralph Branca to give the Giants the pennant, my eyes strayed to another piece and it knocked me out of my chair. It said I was starting in right field in the series opener against Dave Koslo in the stadium the next day.

I didn't believe it. Because, to my way of thinking, Stengel would go with the same line-up and pitchers that knocked off the Red Sox in the double-header for the pennant. You can say what you want about Casey's juggling but if you look back, you'll see he used the same line-up—and batting order—in both games against Boston. And Stengel never forgets a line-up—win, lose, or tie.

Dad, sick and pale, read it, too. In fact, he was so sure the Yanks would repeat that he drove up from Commerce with a friend and arrived in time to take in the Giant-Dodger humdingers. Dad, of course, gave his thanks to the Almighty that I was going to start a World Series, his life's ambition. But his son all but lost his supper. I was ten times tighter than I was when I played my first big league game.

With Dad in town, I stayed with him and Ralph Compton, the Commerce neighbor who came up for the series. Like all of us country folk, Compton wanted to see the sights. So we got up bright and early for a drive down Broadway and up Fifth Avenue. I still was as shaky as a knuckle ball on a drunk and didn't care for the ride. Dad talked me into it, figuring Ralph and the big city buildings would relax me.

It not only relaxed me but I never stopped laughing. Before I reached the stadium, I was loose as fresh sawdust. Mr. Compton had given me one of my biggest belly laughs. As we passed Radio City, he spotted the figure of the big, bronze Atlas and shouted, "I've got to write back home about this! Look! The Statue of Liberty!"

So I played the first game and felt as if I didn't belong. Koslo shut me out and beat us, 5–1. Monty Irvin went all out with four hits in that one and wouldn't stop. I got to thinking that this club, fired up by Leo Durocher, was going to smoke not only for the rest of the month but from here

on. They played as if they knew they were going to win—
or so it seemed. I remember somebody saying, "Those Giants
are playing like the Yankees—against the Yankees."

I was afraid to peek at the line-up for the next game, but
when I finally mustered up the courage and stole a look,
there I was in right field and leading off again. Then I got
my first series hit in the first inning by dragging one left-
handed off Larry Jensen. Lopat needed it like old Zincore,
what with his five-hitter.

I struck out in the third, the Giants went down in order
in the fifth, and I returned to right. Willie Mays led off.
Heard a lot about him during my short stay in the Association. How he raised the roof at Minneapolis, hitting nothing
but .477 in 35 games. Naturally the Giants had recalled him
before I showed up at Kansas City.

We played Mays, a right-hand hitter, to pull. I wasn't over
far enough and moved a few steps more toward left after
somebody's arm in the Yankee dugout wagged me over
there. Then Willie connected. He didn't pull. The drive,
high and hard and in a hurry, shot for right center—between
Di Maggio and me. It was in my territory, at least a lot closer
to me than it was to Joe.

Seeing that the ball was beginning to sink, I gave it everything I had. When I was about ten feet, maybe closer, from
the ball, I noticed Joe circling wide to his left to back me up.
Di Mag had given me the green light to go and get it. Then
it hit me. I heard a loud snap and felt as if I had been
paralyzed.

I started tumbling and turning. But not before Di Mag
saw it. He instinctively broke toward me and gloved the
ball almost directly or slightly behind my head. I already
had hit the dirt. Before I passed out, though, I realized why

he'll go down as one of the greatest center fielders who ever lived.

It's then that I understood the greatness of Di Maggio as player or a "money" player, as the writers call him. First, he caught the ball during a split-second emergency. Then he waved for help before he asked me in what I thought was a loud tone for Joe, "What's the matter, kid?"

I started to tell him I thought I had broken my right knee when I drifted away. The next thing I remember after I came to is Gus Mauch (the Yankee trainer) standing over me, yelling for a stretcher. Gus said it was nothing and told me not to worry and he'd have me back in the ball game in nothing flat. That was just about the nicest lie I ever heard.

They lugged me off to Lenox Hill Hospital where I learned that I had injured a lot of ligaments. They also told me to forget about the rest of the series as far as playing was concerned, and hauled in a television set to make things easier. Nobody had to tell me I was all done for the time-being, but I never dreamed getting that knee in shape again was going to be a five-month grind.

I'd like to give you a little more on Di Maggio. There have been rumors that a "certain coolness" existed between us. One report said that Joe never was seen talking to me. That's correct. And Di Maggio, so far as I know, doesn't do much talking to anybody.

That's why I liked him. He never talked and always minded his own business, including baseball. I like quiet people because I was brought up among people who never said anything unless they had something to say. And when Joe had something to say, he just said it.

There's no need to say so, but Joe had everything and is headed for the Hall of Fame. I liked best his swing. It's about the only thing which could stop me from switch-hitting if I figured I could master it—left or right. But I know I can't.

Dad accompanied me to the hospital after the second-game injury that night and "rented" a bed in the same room. "My back's acting up again," he alibied, "and the rest might do me some good. Besides, I've got to watch that knee of yours."

I smiled and acted dumb. A doctor told me Dad was suffering from cancer of the stomach.

14

Three Dates—and Out

Dad and I stuck around New York—in the hospital—for another week. Dr. Gaynor braced up my knee, told me to take it easy, and we headed back for Commerce. I looked forward to seeing my girl Merlyn, watching the twins play football and basketball, wrestling with Butch, and going hunting and fishing.

I'd like to tell you what led up to my marriage at the age of twenty. It all started one November night in 1950. I had a date with a gal named Lavanda Whipkey. I was taking her to a football game at Picher where Picher played Fairland in a big county game. Preston Christman came along with us for the ride. Pres had a date with one of Picher's drum majorettes—second in command. She said her name was Merlyn Johnson.

So I met Merlyn and began to switch-hit romantically, if you can call it that. I went hook, line, sinker, pole, and bait for Miss Johnson. Man, she was pretty. I asked Pres if he minded if I asked her for a date. He said he didn't. Mama puts it this way:

"All Mickey needed was that one date to fall for Merlyn. It was about midnight when he strolled in on this particular night. He looked as if he was floating. Mickey didn't appear ailing and, yet, he seemed he needed some kind of doctoring. Then I knew what the trouble was when Mickey got mushy and babbled it out, 'I met the cutest little thing in Picher tonight. She twirls one of the batons for the Picher band. She's got freckles, reddish hair, and is no taller than that.' I recognized the symptoms, counted it off as a heavy case of puppy love, and let it go that.

"But I was wrong. They had one date, then two and three dates. Mickey struck out on the third date. After that one, he confided to me he had asked Merlyn to be his steady and she had agreed. I knew it was only a matter of time until their marriage. Mickey, as the city folk say, was really gone."

That just about explains how Merlyn and I got together. She and my brothers made it a lot easier for me, because Dad kept getting worse all the time and my right knee wasn't getting any stronger. I took Dad to the Mayo Clinic in Rochester, Minnesota, and they confirmed what we had known all the time.

Right here I'd like to tell you something about Ray and Roy. In my book, they're future all-Americans in both football and basketball and can't miss reaching the big leagues as ball-players. I believe they'd like to wind up as professionals in baseball but, at the same time, nothing is going to stop them from playing football and basketball. The college that gets them is going to be lucky.

As ball-players with the Commerce Tigers, Ray, a left-hand hitter, is a first baseman and Roy, an outfielder, is a right-hand hitter. They decided to leave the switch-hitting up to me. Both are very fast and, as I said before, probably can outrun me. I like to dream of seeing an all-Mantle outfield some day.

The River Street Mantles (that's our immediate branch) aren't the only athletic-minded Mantles in Commerce. I've got two cousins, Max and Ronnie Mantle, who are right up there with Ray and Roy. Although not as tall, they're tougher than ten tons of tailings. (That's what's left after the zinc and lead have been extracted.)

Besides starring in football and in basketball, Max and Ronnie are baseball whangs. Max is a shortstop and Ronnie, an outfielder. Which reminds me, I still owe those boys a couple of Yankee caps. Ray and Roy have them and wear them to church, school, and every place else.

Here's their daily schedule during the school season. Breakfast, hunting, school, lots of lunch, school, practice in the seasonal sport, hunting, and supper. And if I said that used to be my routine, I'd be telling the truth. I still do the hunting and eating part with them but it's getting expensive. I have to furnish most of the shells. We have a gun apiece and Larry, the youngest, tags along with an air rifle. He's a nice kid but Mama may send him to reform school —he plays football in the house.

Which reminds me that the house at 317 River Street is now *our home*. We paid off the mortgage with my series share and I'm glad I was voted a full one. We needed the money, with Dad ailing and me getting married. But it's a neat, comfortable seven-room cottage with plenty of space for our family. The telephone number is 318-W. Two rings mean us.

So we owned the house but, all the time, I didn't have a

leg to stand on. I kept brooding about my bum knee, especially since it was beginning to act as if it was never going
to heal. I even had to rest after what I thought was a short
walk in the woods. It reminded me of osteomyelitis all over
again which, thank heaven, remained in an arrested state as
long as I continued taking the periodic treatments.

As a result, I had two legs to worry about. What puzzled
me was that I never had experienced the slightest kind of
trouble with either knee until that accident in the 1951 series.
I still don't know how or why it happened unless I "stopped
too short," as somebody pointed out to me later. I didn't
know what to think and, once in a while, wondered if it was
osteomyelitis spreading to others parts of my body.

The fall and winter of 1951 and the first two months of
1952 were the toughest I ever experienced, if you add it all
up. Dad got sicker and sicker and finally he couldn't work
at the mines. My right knee was healing too slowly for me,
with spring training just around the corner. And I wanted
to play center field since Di Maggio announced his re-
tirement.

I thought a lot about Di Maggio, and thinking about him
eased my own problems. As every kid knows, Joe started
out with the Yankees as a gamble in 1936, because he was
supposed to have a trick knee—even though he had just hit
.398 in 172 games with San Francisco in the Pacific Coast
League the year before. And, of course, I knew all about
those operations for the removal of bone spurs in each heel,
starting in 1947. And I secretly hoped to shake off my injuries as he had. I sincerely believe that Di Maggio's were a
lot tougher than mine.

Most of the Yankee stars, past and present, were broken

up badly somewhere along the line. Phil Rizzuto almost lost a leg as a result of a spike injury his first year at Bassets in the Bi-State League in 1937. Tommy Henrich had everything but a broken neck. Hank Bauer fought with the Marines in the Pacific and was wounded on Okinawa during the World War II. Ralph Houk served as a major in the Rangers in the European theater. Jerry Coleman piloted a dive bomber for the Marines, and now he's flying jets for the Marines in Korea. Johnny Mize beat all kinds of leg and arm injuries.

I didn't have to tell Stengel about my knee. He took one look and told me to take it easy. I had to, too. My 1952 contract had some knee "ifs" in it, and my fitness hinged on it from a standpoint of money. What a difference a year had made. Practically a forgotten man, in my case.

The papers had everybody going out for center field: Woodling, Bauer, Jensen, and Bob Cerv, up from Kansas City who really was belting them "fer pieces" in the exhibitions. While I hoped the best man would win, I might as well be honest—I wanted to be the Yankee center fielder. No other position would satisfy me, but from the looks of things I'd be lucky to make the squad.

My running—or limping—never fooled Stengel. He'd take a look and change the subject. I finally made it in the spring exhibitions by pinch-hitting for Frank Shea and forcing Andy Carey at third. I mention the force play because I was withdrawn for a runner. Casey knew the score, although he told me he was "playing it safe to get that knee in shape." I was really going places—in reverse.

So I pinch-hit and pinch-hit and pinch-hit and guys would run for me. I played in the outfield, in right, for the first time in St. Petersburg on March 18. We played the Braves and I replaced Archie Wilson in the fifth inning. Got in nine innings, anyway. The Braves beat us, 1–0, in fourteen innings on straight doubles by Sam Jethroe and George Bruton. Spahan, Donovan, and Burdette combined a five-hitter, one fewer than given up by Raschi, Morgan, Kuzava, and Ostrowski. Some ball game.

Yet, I was thankful for that overtime game. Those last nine against the Braves encouraged me and convinced Stengel that my knee was slowly but surely coming around. The next day I opened and finished in right against the Phillies in Clearwater. Roberts and Ridzik held us to two hits. Luckily I got both of them—a homer and a single. We lost, 8–1.

But it still was right field for me all through Florida. I enjoyed my happiest day of the spring in Atlanta on April 5. I started in center field for the first time and continued playing in the middle through Columbus, Georgia, and Norfolk, Virginia. Then it was Jensen and Cerv the rest of the northern trip through Baltimore and the series against the Dodgers.

I opened the 1952 season against the A's in Philly in right field. Jensen played center and Bauer, left. Raschi, relieved by Sain in the ninth, won, 8–1. I got three hits including a two-run double off Carl Sheib in a five-run ninth inning and felt pretty good, mostly because I made four put-outs during the first three innings. Opened up to catch a drive by Ferris Fain in the first, with no damage resulting.

Meanwhile I remained in right as Jensen, Woodling, and Cerv alternated in center. That was the pattern through April. Then the Yanks pulled what the papers called a "big deal." Jensen, Shea, and Wilson went to Washington for Irv Noren. On May 3, Noren played his first game as the Yankee center fielder in the stadium against the White Sox.

I still was the gimpy-legged right fielder.

15

On My Own

Dad died in a Denver hospital on May 6, 1952.

Although I . . . the whole family . . . had known for some months that his passing would be only a matter of time, his loss left me with a strange lonesomeness. I had the feeling of being a little boy all over again . . . his hand reaching out to lead me to ball games and teaching and preaching baseball to me as far back as I could remember. Somehow, though, the hand was still there, and kids who grew up with fathers as I did know what I'm trying to say.

The Indians were in town when I got the news. A night game was scheduled in the stadium and I knew Dad would have wanted me to play. The fellows were especially nice to me and Stengel was particularly understanding. He wanted to know if I had gotten in touch with my mother because there had been some trouble getting through to Commerce on the telephone.

Casey told me not to return until "you feel good and ready." He then cheered me up, actually making me grin by cracking something about needing me something awful or something like that. Stengel wasn't kidding me, though. The Sunday before in a double-header against the White Sox I had gone 1–for–9 and dropped to .258.

All of Dad's friends from the tristate area were there for his funeral. Miners, merchants, farmers, and, of course, all his buddies who had argued baseball with him the whole year around. On the way to the cemetery we passed the very spot where he started to teach me to switch-hit. What struck me as odd was that a little kid was in the same yard batting out a baseball. And from the way Dad scored, it was a double.

You'll have to forgive me if this sounds dramatic, but I returned from the funeral a different person, if not a ballplayer. Up to Dad's death, baseball had been a game. Sure, I liked the money but I never thought of it too seriously. Now it was a profession. I had to put on the overalls for Mama, the twins, Barbara, Larry, and my wife. I had to make it, and felt that I would.

I was back in the stadium against the Red Sox on May 11. From left to right, it was Bauer, Noren, and me. My right knee, as if by some secret cure, began to feel better. I could open up on the bases as well as in the field. We hit the road, opening in Cleveland on Tuesday night, May 13. It's a night that handed me my number one stunner and not because the Indians let us have it, 10–6.

At the beginning of the game I watched from the bench, but I was in there at the fifth inning—*at third base*. Stengel just stuck me in there for Bobby Brown. I never knew—or asked—why. Casey, let's say, was just in one of his moods. Another good reason I didn't get too inquisitive after it was all over is that I fielded .500, two errors in four chances. It was certainly a long way from center field, I thought.

After the game I sounded out a veteran with whom I was eating, and all he replied was, "Mickey, when you've been around as long as I have in this business, you'll mark it down as just another day and let it go at that. The best way to second-guess your manager is to keep chewing your gum." He then chuckled. "Didn't you know that anybody who is connected with professional baseball is crazy?" For a minute I almost believed him.

So I "chewed my gum" for the next four games as Gil McDougald played third and I played "last" on the bench. Both Collins and Mize were hurt at the time and Noren, who used to play first base in the minor leagues and occasionally for the Senators, played first base. Bob Cerv played center.

We were in Chicago on May 20 when I believe it was Billy Martin who signaled to me that I was not only in the line-up as the center fielder but batting third in the line-up. I enjoyed my first four-hit day of the year and got two singles, left-handed, off Ken Holcombe and two singles, right-handed, off Chuck Stobbs. Johnny Sain pitched a six-hitter for a 3–1 win.

Those four jumped my average to .315 and I intended to keep it over .300 the rest of the way. I stayed hot and by June 3 had reached .333, thanks to another four-hit day, right-handed, against Billy Pierce and the White Sox. Collins broke it with a single in the thirteenth inning to score me for a 4–3 win.

I knew I had to keep on hitting to remain in center. Luckily I've been there ever since, although I got the shakes again when I slumped to .290 on June 21. I pulled back over .300 in a double-header the next day and managed to sink no more than four below the rest of the season. I finished the year with .311.

Our last Western trip, by way of Philadelphia and Washington, did it, but even writing about it still chills me. Besides series with the A's and Senators, there were two at St. Louis, two at Chicago, the one great big one at Cleveland, and two at Detroit. Since the opposing managers were saving their ace pitchers for the Yankee visits, we were doped to fall apart after this one.

Ewell Blackwell and Johnny Sain shut out the Red Sox, 2–0, in the stadium on the night of September 2 and we shoved off three and a half games in front. They said it was a fair cushion but a little too thin for comfort. I began to understand when Jimmy Dykes treated us to Harry Byrd who shut us out, 3–1, on a beautiful one-hitter on Irv Noren's second-inning double.

Gil McDougald evened it up for us the next night by hitting two homers, one off Shantz, for five RBI's and a 12–2 win. Then Alex Kellner beat us, 3–2, in the third game and our lead shriveled to two and a half games. Nobody seemed to cry. We boarded the train for the short hop to Washington that night (it was September 5) as happy as you please.

I guess I was as happy as the next one. We all piled into the diner, ordered steaks with all the trimmings, and between mouthfuls began playing games—Twenty Questions. It was fun—just made you forget everything. I even guessed a couple of questions myself. They all pertained to sports. I wasn't bad on knowing the all-Americans who came from the Middle West.

Laughs swept from every table except one. That was the one in the center of the car—at which sat Stengel, Crosetti, Dickey, and Turner. The faces of the Crow, Bill, and Jim were as frozen as the Rocky Mountains, but they were eating. Casey's face, paler than old milk, stayed closed.

Stengel wasn't even eating but he certainly was listening. After taking in about a million of the Twenty Questions, he took to the coaching lines. He just stood up when nobody was noticing and the waiters were serving, and really waded into us. I'd better not quote him, but Stengel also had a question: "I got a question to ask you fellers . . . *Who Won Tonight?*"

Then he lit into us. It got so quiet you could hear a baked potato drop. And before we rolled another mile or so, all of us had padded out and hidden in our car. I understand the newspaper guys (who also played a little bit of the Twenty Questions themselves) wrote it up large and fancy. Some of the writers even made jokes about it after they got to Washington. One even kidded me. "Don't look now and don't tell anybody, Mickey, but they're bootlegging Twenty Questions in Room 203-F." At the same time they praised Stengel for calling us down and I guess they were right. Because we woke up and, as it turned out, we stayed awake, thank goodness.

We knocked off the Nats, 5–2 and 5–1, as Johnny Mize pinch-hit a grand-slammer off Walt Masterson in the sixth inning of the second game. Big John, of course, jumped for joy in this one. It was the Cat's first homer in big Griffith Stadium since he came to the Yanks in September, 1949, and it gave him the distinction of hitting a homer in every big league park including Baker Bowl, the old Philadelphia park. Mize's beauty over the high right-field wall enabled us to hold a two-game lead.

We spent the next day rolling halfway across the country to St. Louis and opened a series with the Browns the following night. Clint Courtney was hit by a pitch in the ninth inning with the bases full and we lost, 5–4. It chopped the Yankees' lead to a game. Then Reynolds beat them the next day to protect. It was the beginning of an iron-man role for the Chief.

The Yanks laid off a day, Cleveland won, and on September 11, our three and a half lead had been squeezed to a half-game. We played a pair at Chicago and Mr. Richards was ready. We won them both with Reynolds saving Sain in the second game. That was on September 13. The next day it was a single game with the Indians and I don't have to say any more.

Those two enabled us to head for Cleveland with a one and a half game lead. We were feeling pretty good, everybody except Rizzuto. There was nothing wrong with Phil, physically, but I had him crazy. There are two things Rizzuto can't stand: riding with his back to the engine while on a train and listening to stories, anywhere, about anything that crawls.

I'm not much of a storyteller but, being a 100 per cent country boy, I know plenty about things that crawl, especially snakes—not to mention lizards and skunks. So I decided to give Phil my special water-moccasin-rattler treatment. I told a whopper about how I used to catch poisonous snakes, pull out their fangs with my fingers, and train them for house pets. Phil got so sick he begged, "Please, Mickey, no more snake stories until after the game with the Indians! Wotta you trying to do, make me blow the pennant?"

I let up on Rizzuto and he swears that's why he managed to get a big single in a four-run third off Garcia, more than enough to win for Lopat. That's the game I like to remember best: September 14, in Cleveland. The local papers were loaded with that psychological stuff, and I guess they had something, at that. Over 73,000 turned out for that single game, which is good for Cleveland where they certainly can rustle up the crowds.

I don't call it bragging, but I felt we were going to win as early as the first inning. I doubled off Garcia after two were out. I homered off Lou Brissie in the fifth, but Reynolds was the relief sensation for the second straight day. The Chief relieved Lopat in the sixth and turned on the chill. I said before he was an artist and I'll say it again. Reynolds is the favorite of the favorites. No, Stengel and Turner never told me. They just look that way.

We left town two and a half games in front and held it as we beat the Tigers twice in Detroit. In the opener, Bill Miller shut them out, 7–0, with a three-hitter. Collins homered and singled off Art Houtteman and singled off Billy Hoeft, and Bauer singled off Houtteman and homered off Hoeft.

And we got even with Virgil Trucks the next day, 12–3. Bauer homered and hit two singles and I homered and doubled twice for the day. I say "even" with Trucks because Virgil is the same guy who no-hit us in New York on August 25 for his second of the year after doing it to the Senators in Detroit on May 15 to tie Reynolds' American League record set in 1951.

Jimmy Dykes "saved" Shantz for us as we returned to New York on the nineteenth and Bobby shut us out, 2–0, cutting our lead down to a game and a half again. Lopat handed the A's the same kind of 2–0 treatment and Reynolds followed it up with a 1–0 job. And that's why we stayed on top.

Incidentally it was during this particular three-hitter by

Allie, on September 21, that I landed right squarely into the Yankee record books. Red Patterson, I'm told, calls it a "negative statistic." Anyway, Mr. Harry Byrd struck me out swinging, my first time up in the second inning that was for Mickey Mantle, strike-out number 106.

So I quietly replaced Frankie Crosetti on the "honor roll" who held the distinction since 1937 for fanning 105 times, as I said before. And as I also said before, I wound up with 111. Just how Berra was held to twelve strike-outs in 1950, also a Yankee record for the fewest number of strike-outs, I'll never know.

Walter Masterson fanned me four straight times in Washington on August 6 and in Chicago, on September 13, Marv Grissom struck me out three times in a row. I'm an authority on the subject.

Why do I strike out so often? A good question. And I think I know some of the answers. Plainly speaking, it's because I like to hit homers and I swing with everything I've got. That's not always the best way to win ball games, and I keep promising myself, in the future, I'll go for the base hit if and when it means the difference. I still can hear Casey in such situations pleading, "Just meet the ball, that's all." Of course, I must do more than that to cut down on my strike-outs.

Still, I resent the criticism from some that I strike out so often just because I'm fooled. That's not altogether correct. It's mostly because I go for the long ball. However, when you see me look or swing and miss a 3–2 pitch, just let it go that the pitcher has made a sucker out of me again.

About the only thing that can take the bad taste of strike-outs out of this book is talking a little bit about homers. I got some fan mail wanting to know the longest hit I believe I made in the big leagues.

I think I hit my longest homer, right-handed, off Hoeft in Detroit on June 17, 1952. They tell me the drive landed in the upper deck of the left-center bleachers in Briggs Stadium. I think I hit my longest, left-handed, off Early Wynn in Yankee Stadium on July 15, 1952. Bill Dickey swears it sailed "way up yonder" in the right-center field bleachers.

I think the hardest I ever hit was in Detroit on September 17 off Bill Wight, who had been traded from the Red Sox to the Tigers. Although I batted right-handed, this one landed in the right-field stands. I hit that one and it disappeared. I felt *good!*

The most thrilling homer I ever hit in my life was in Chicago on the night of July 29, 1952. It was my grand-slammer, right-handed, off Chuck Stobbs in the ninth inning that beat the White Sox, 10–7.

My ambition is to homer from each side during the same game. I've done it during the same day but never during the same game. On July 13, 1952, in a double-header against the Tigers in the stadium, I homered, left-handed, off Marlin Stuart in the opener and homered, right-handed, off Hal Newhouser in the second game.

John Lingo, who coached me at Commerce High and now is on the coaching staff at Miami (Oklahoma) high, says I homered from each side during a high school game. I don't remember, but I'm sure it never happened since I've been in pro ball.

16

Making the Main Drag

Champagne was on the house the night of September 26 in Philadelphia. That's when the Yankees made it four straight for Stengel. The bottles, however, had two innings of extra ice. That's because we didn't win it until the eleventh inning when Billy Martin broke it up with a two-run single off Harry Byrd to wrap it for Johnny Sain, 5–2.

Sain, as you know, didn't get his tobacco to squirting until the ninth when he took over for Ed Lopat. Lope had a 2–0 shut-out for five and then Gus Zernial wiped it out with a two-run homer in the sixth. Talk about a guy who can send them sailing—what about Zeke? And for left-handed power, check on Luke Easter's muscles.

Irv Noren gave us our first run with a homer in the third and I got hold of one in the fourth for our second. It was my last homer of the regular season and I don't mind telling you it made me feel pretty good to hit it off Byrd. Harry is tough. Which reminds me, the series with the A's probably would have been a lot tougher if Bobby Shantz hadn't broken his left wrist just three days before this ball game.

95

One of the nice things about the fancy drinks (only for pennants) and the juicy cuts at our Hotel Warwick party was meeting Frank Leahy, Notre Dame coach, who dropped in to pay his respects. Notre Dame was playing Penn the next day. Being an Oklahoma fan, naturally, and knowing the Sooners were to show in South Bend later in the season, I asked Leahy how he thought he'd do against O.U.

Leahy told me he thought Oklahoma had one of the strongest teams in the nation and he'd be lucky to hold them to a respectable score. He sounded as if he meant it and he could see I leaned a little toward the Sooners. My off-season boss, Harold Youngman, flew me up to South Bend in his private plane to see Oklahoma kill them. That Leahy! From now on, I'm going to ask him how he feels and let it go at that. It's a lot smarter.

But we had a good time in the Warwick that night and the next one, too, because we had two more games with the A's before the end of the regular season. Talking about our hotels, they're all great. In addition to the swanky Shoreham in Washington and the Warwick in Philly, there's the Kenmore in Boston, Del Prado, right on Lake Michigan in Chicago, Wade Park Manor in Cleveland, Book Sheraton in Detroit, and the Chase in St. Louis. Of course, the nicest thing about them is that you don't pay—you just sign. And I won't be bashful in nominating the club's heaviest eater —me.

The Yankee hotels around the circuit are a little better than the ones that quartered us, say, in the KOM League. I used to do a little bell-hopping, on the side, at the Main Hotel in Miami. And there's a nice fellow who knows plenty about baseball clerking at the Hotel Miami right now. He's Jack Killilay, who pitched for the Red Sox in 1911. Jack is full of stories of when he barnstormed through Japan early in the century. But there are times when I think we had more fun traveling in the smaller towns, stopping at the smaller hotels. That is, if you call having water and pillow fights with your roommates fun.

It got us in trouble in Ponca City, Oklahoma, once. A fire broke out in one of the rooms on our floor. It would be tattling to tell whose room it was in. We all turned firemen, snatching the hose off the wall and pouring it on and maybe drowning a few innocent people. The manager threatened to call the police if we didn't move. It took Harry Craft all night to cool the manager off.

I haven't much to say about the 1952 World Series. First, I appreciate what Jackie Robinson had to say about the part I played in it, but somehow you don't talk about the Yankees unless you mean the whole team. But if you ask me who were important, I'd say Allie Reynolds, Johnny Mize, Bob Kuzava, and Billy Martin, who caught Robinson's windblown pop fly in the sixth of the seventh game. Where did he catch it, anyway—on the mound, at the plate, or at the third-base line? I wouldn't know. I was backed up against the left-center fence.

Homering off Joe Black in the sixth of the deciding game that gave us a lead and singling off Preacher Roe in the seventh for our fourth run thrilled me plenty, I must confess. But I didn't enjoy it until Gene Woodling caught Pee Wee Reese's long fly for the last out. Also got a big kick out of the fact that Commerce took a day off to watch the series by television. Moreland Brothers Hardware and Furniture Store, in the center of Commerce, put up a set right out on the sidewalk and tuned in on Tulsa.

It came in clearly, they say, but it caused a revolution

among the kids in grade school. They weren't allowed to watch and that included my younger brother, Butch. It made him so mad he broke out of school three different times. But they'd always bring him back after a couple of innings. The twins and Barbara, of course, were eligible to watch since they were in high school.

I'm too green to be in the "experts" business but I'm old enough to throw bouquets. Just want to say this about the Brooklyn Dodgers. They're good, with an outfield that's just —well—great. Better not say anything too nice about Charley Dressen's fly-catchers in front of Mize. You might escape with your life if you mention Duke Snider or Andy Pafko; but for the sake of your health, don't even think of Carl Furillo. At that, it seems Carl used a pair of frog's legs when he robbed the Cat in the eleventh of the fifth game. Remember?

I couldn't get back to Commerce, 1,400 miles away, fast enough after the series. It ended on a Tuesday. Cleaned up my business that night. I threw Mama and Merlyn in the car early Wednesday morning and off we went. We only took time out for food and gas and reached Commerce Thursday night, nonstop from Richmond, Indiana, at the half. I mean after the first two quarters of the football game between Commerce and Picher. I was about fifteen minutes too late: Ray already had ripped off a 96-yard touchdown. Commerce won, 13–0. Ray outscored Roy for the year because Roy broke his leg during the middle of the season. He's O.K. now.

That made it a perfect homecoming. And one of the persons I was most happy to see was Grandma Anna. That's Mrs. Anna Richardson, seventy-four years old, who came over from Spavinaw to take care of the house while Mama and Merlyn were at the series. Grandma Anna is a baseball fan, too. She also taught—or forced me—how to mop and wash dishes. That's when Mama was sick and I was about eight years old.

Several days after I had returned home, Ott Chandler left his drugstore and came over to the house. Ott, a friend of the family for years, hemmed and hawed about an hour. I knew something was on his mind and I finally asked what it was. That's all Ott was waiting for.

"Well, Mickey," began Ott, "this is what ails me. You're not going to like it, but I'd appreciate it if you'd do it. Speaking in behalf of the Commerce Lions Club, we want to throw a parade in your honor. It's all arranged. All you have to do is get in a car with Merlyn, ride down Main Street, and attend a banquet. You won't have to make any speeches. I knew you'd agree."

Meanwhile I had gotten myself a job, or had one given me, I should say. As I said before, Harold Youngman looked me up on the recommendation of Barney Barnett. Not only did Mr. Youngman make me a wonderful proposition so far as money is concerned, but he gave me a chance to learn the contracting business. We build roads, and it keeps me outdoors—which I like.

I might as well confess that Harold isn't planning on killing me with work. He owns his own hunting lodge and urges me to spend most of my "working" time using it. Mr. Youngman just throws me the keys and tells me to take over. And he, by the way, is no tenderfoot in the field-and-stream sports himself.

You should see the office and desk he gave me. There's a name-plate and everything. Makes me feel like the president of a corporation. Mr. Youngman has given me only one "order" since I've been working for him. He advised me to answer my fan mail. I don't need a secretary to handle it, but I'm flattered by the number of letters I get.

I even got one from an astrologist. He said I was born under the sign of Libra and told me I was "very unorthodox with good mental equilibrium." And . . . "It accounts for your switch-hitting characteristics, and your horoscope is packed with dynamite so far as activity is concerned." I asked Mr. Youngman to answer it for me and he said he might consider it after he talked with his lawyer.

It was quite a parade on Friday, October 17, 1952. The main drag was dressed up with all kinds of "Welcome Home" banners. Ott decorated his drugstore windows with write-ups about me that he clipped out of magazines and papers. And district bands and drum corps from all over Ottawa County paraded. They said about 7,000 persons attended, the first parade held in Commerce since World War I. Here's a write-up about it from the Miami *Daily News-Record*:

"Notables from the baseball world lavished high praise on Mickey Mantle at a banquet honoring the Yankee World Series hero with 450 Mantle fans on hand. Allie Reynolds, Yankee pitcher, Tom Greenwade, Yankee scout who discovered him, and Joe Becker, old-time umpire, player, and baseball authority, all expressed opinions that Mantle might become one of the greatest baseball players ever to perform.

"The banquet, staged at the old Spartan Cafeteria, climaxed a full day for the youthful No. 1 citizen of Commerce. A parade Friday morning with an estimated 7,000 looking on, and afternoon football game were included in the day's activities. At the banquet, Mickey was presented with a commodore and colonel's commission from Governor Johnston Murray. Mantle is the only person to hold both commissions.

"The sponsoring Commerce Lions club gave Mickey and his wife, Merlyn, a set of sterling silver. Master of ceremonies was Arthur H. Hottel. The flag salute was led by Paul Wheelen and Pearl Mason gave the invocation. Mayor Arthur Peck presented his appreciation to everybody with his response.

"Ott Chandler, general chairman of the Lions Club 'Mantle Day' Committee, introduced special visitors. These included Judge Haywood Scott of Joplin; E. L. Dale, KOM League president; Barney Barnett, who started Mickey on his career; Lloyd Lee, Lions Club president; Dr. Bruce G. Carter, S. A. Robertson, and Homa Thomas of Northeastern A. & M., colleges and Mrs. Allie Reynolds.

"Mantle's family was introduced by E. V. Miller. The family included Mickey's mother, Mrs. E. C. Mantle; three brothers, Roy, Ray, and Larry; sister, Barbara, and uncle and aunt, Mr. and Mrs. Emmett Mantle."

I made a speech: "Thanks to everybody!" which is pretty good for me.

Later that night I excused myself, jumped into the car, and drove to the GAR cemetery. I snapped off the lights and started from the beginning. From switch-hitting at tennis balls to the Peewee League . . . high school and the Ban Johnson League. Osteomyelitis, Greenwade and the Yankee contract . . . Independence and Joplin. My rookie year with the Yanks at Phoenix and my start in the big leagues . . . my demotion to Kansas City and back to the Yanks. My injury in the 1951 World Series and being together in the same hospital room . . . and his death.

The grass covering Dad's grave was fresh and green—unusually green, I thought, for the middle of October.

And I don't believe I ever saw the moon shining more brightly.

17

Ben Epstein: What About Mantle's Future?

Ted McGrew, veteran scout of the Boston Red Sox, addressed the second annual dinner and meeting of the San Diego (California) Hot Stove League on November 20, 1952. McGrew lauded Mickey Mantle of the Yankees as a perfect example of a player who never stopped hustling even after he made good in the majors.

"Here is a player," said Ted, "who, in my estimation, is greater than Joe Di Maggio ever was. He got that way because he didn't let down once he got to the Big Time.

"Mantle is faster, a better hitter, and has a better arm than Di Maggio. With two strikes on Mantle, the infield naturally is playing back and Mickey is so fast you just don't make a play on him when he bunts unless he sends one right back to the mound."

Coming from McGrew or Joe Doaks, that's a mouthful.

Hundreds of experts beg to differ that Mantle shouldn't be mentioned in the same argument when compared to

Di Maggio. Not now, anyway. After all, Joe stood the test of time, whereas Mickey qualified as a bona-fide big league star for only one season—1952.

Yet, Mantle reflects greatness in every department. He already has established himself as the finest switch-hitter in the history of the game. Frankie Frisch was the best of the left-right batters up to now, but the old Fordham Flash isn't in the same class with the young man from Commerce, Oklahoma.

Mantle's qualifications to attain the heights of hitting, unlimited (from either side), stand out in bold relief. Mickey has the might, the form, and the ambition or hustle, so keenly observed by Mr. McGrew.

Ever since he played ball at Joplin as an eighteen-year-old, Mickey's bat signalized the tremendous lofting and driving power as illustrated by Babe Ruth, Jimmy Foxx, Lou Gehrig, Ted Williams, and others. On the other hand, he has shown the flaming hitting consistency of a Ty Cobb, Rogers Hornsby, Paul Waner, George Sisler, Hans Wagner, Tris Speaker, Stan Musial, Di Maggio, and others.

It's too early, of course, to classify Mantle defensively with the Speakers, Di Maggios, and Terry Moores. Still, as Casey Stengel says, "The kid is catching on out there in center field and with that speed, no telling what he'll be able to catch with a little more experience. He can throw a baseball farther than anybody. Look out, if he learns how to control it and that's what he's learning."

But will Mickey hold up physically? That's the $64 question. He suffers from osteomyelitis on his left shin. After grading him 4-F twice because of a bone disease, army surgeons rejected him a third time on account of a bad right knee (1951 World Series injury) only last December, 1952.

If Mickey is able to play ball over a number of seasons, without serious physical handicap, you can put it down in your book that he'll probably write himself a ticket to Cooperstown. I say probably, because you can never tell. Out of the hundreds of phenoms that have crossed the threshold of the major leagues in the past twenty years, maybe ten have been names you'd remember. Out of those ten, perhaps three attained real stardom. In my opinion, Mickey Charles Mantle is one man in three: a super star of the future.

Appendix

In line with Mantle's "Yankee tomorrow," Red Patterson has compiled some interesting figures. It's baseball's general theory that rookies who deliver in their sophomore year and break through the so-called "jinx" barrier usually rocket to stardom. Mickey's jump (excluding his Kansas City mark) represented a 44-point increase from .267 in 1951 to .311 in 1952.

"With few exceptions," pointed out Patterson, "nearly all the game's greatest hitters lifted their batting marks in their sophomore years, but only a handful ever showed a 44-point improvement as did Mantle."

Following are the statistics on some of the stars, past and present, showing how their percentages grew in their second year. Babe Ruth was a notable exception, hitting .315 in his first year and .272 in his second, but baseball's home run champion was a pitcher at the time. In his first year as a regular, everyday outfielder, Ruth hit .322 and zoomed to .375 the next.

Sophomore-year Percentages of Famous Ball-players

	First Year	Second Year
Ty Cobb (.367)	.320	.350
Rogers Hornsby (.358)	.313	.357
Lou Gehrig (.340)	.295	.313
George Sisler (.340)	.285	.305
Stan Musial (.348)	.315	.357
Ted Williams (.347)	.327	.344
Tris Speaker (.345)	.309	.340
Charley Gehringer (.313)	.277	.317
Joe Di Maggio (.325)	.323	.346
Johnny Mize (.313)	.329	.364
Frankie Frisch (.316)	.226	.280
Joe Medwick (.324)	.318	.319
Jimmy Foxx (.327)	.313	.323
Zack Wheat (.317)	.284	.287
Nap Lajoie (.338)	.328	.363
Bill Dickey (.316)	.324	.339

Mantle's Lifetime Batting Averages

Year	Club	League	Pos.	G	AB	R	H	2B	3B	HR	RBI	PCT
1949	Independence	KOM	SS	89	323	54	101	15	7	7	63	.313
1950	Joplin	W.A.	SS	137	519	141	199	30	12	26	136	.383
1951	New York	A.L.	OF	96	341	61	91	11	5	13	65	.267
1951	Kansas City	A.A.	OF	40	166	32	60	9	3	11	50	.361
1952*	New York	A.L.	OF	142	549	94	171	37	7	23	87	.311

* Right-handed: 74 hits in 222 times at bat. Left-handed: 97 hits in 327 times at bat.

World Series Averages

Year	Club	League	Pos.	G	AB	R	H	2B	3B	HR	RBI	PCT
1951	New York	A.L.	OF	2	5	1	1	0	0	0	0	.200
1952	New York	A.L.	OF	7	29	5	10	1	1	2	3	.345

UNITED PRESS PHOTO

Here's a picture taken during spring training in 1950.

From left to right: Hank Bauer, me, and Gene Woodling.

Another spring training photo.

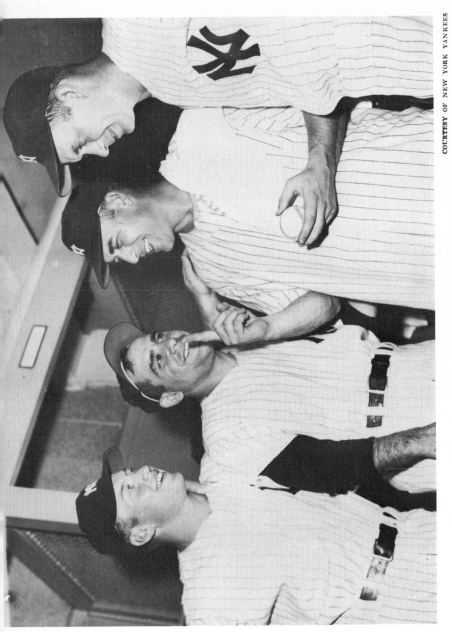

Here are a bunch of us talking it up after Vic Raschi had just chucked a one-hitter.

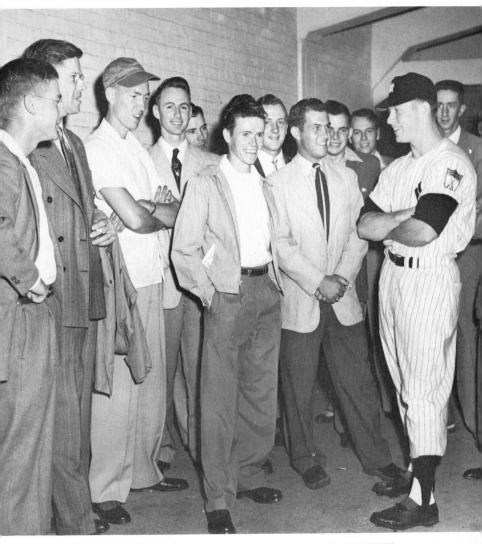

The Esso Standard Oil Company gave these fellows scholarships and topped them off with a free graduation trip to New York. They are all 4-H boys.

Ted Williams kids me at batting practice.

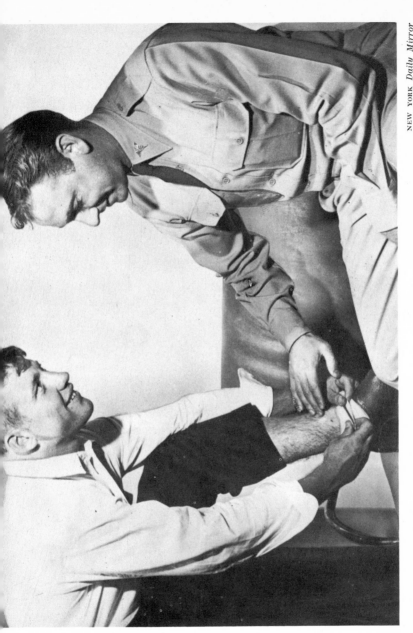

Captain George Farrell examines me in Oklahoma City. Because of my osteomyelitis I was classified 4-F.

I get a single during a game with the Brooklyn Dodgers during April, 1951, exhibition game.

Joe Di Maggio, me, and Ted Williams in April, 1951.

George Selkirk, manager of the Kansas City Blues, talks to me in a pregame huddle at Borchert Field in Milwaukee before a game with the Brewers.

I rejoin the Yankees in Cleveland, after being sent down to K.C.

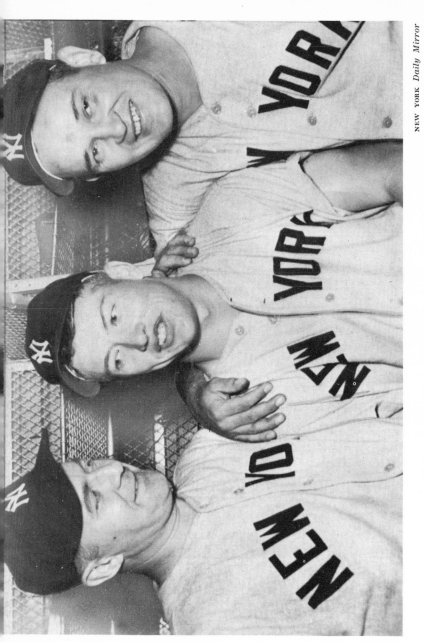

Hubbub after we beat the Indians, 7–3, on August 25, 1951.

From left to right: me, Gene Woodling, Bobby Brown, Yogi Berra, and Gil McDougald. We all hit home runs against Washington on September 9, 1951.

Feller, a tough pitcher any day anywhere, serves one up to me on September 16, 1951. Yes, I swung—and flied out.

Sometimes, even when you give it everything you have, you can't make the grade. If that gate had been open, I probably would have walked up into the stands. But Ed Robinson of the White Sox banged the ball too hard. It was a homer.

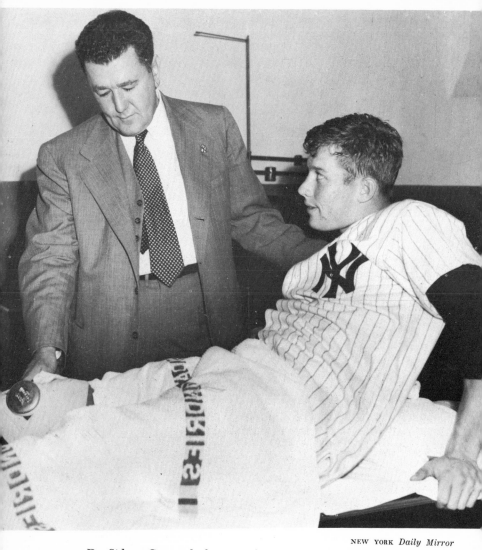

Dr. Sidney Gaynor looks at my knee. I hurt it in the second game of
the 1951 World Series, chasing a Willie Mays fly. We won 3–1.

I was twice as miserable as I look here.

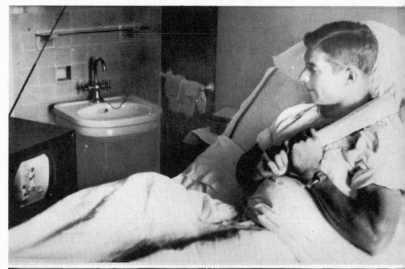

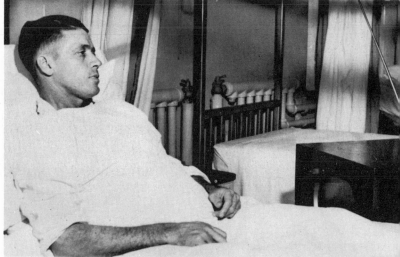

Dad and I watch the third game on TV at Lenox Hill Hospital. The Yanks lost, 6–2.

My brothers Ray (right) and Roy after winning a game for Commerce High. They're still growing, too.

Here's Merlyn, my wife, and me taken in December, 1951.

I love to hunt, and here's proof of it.

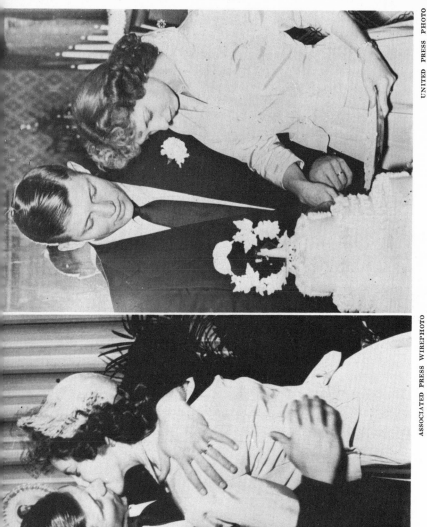

Wedding cake.

December 23, 1951, was a big day for me. Merlyn and I were married at her folks' home in Picher.

This was taken shortly before the wedding. From left to right: Roy, me, Mama, Larry, Dad, and Ray.

A picture taken during spring training, 1952.

We beat the Athletics, 5–2, and clinch the 1952 American League pennant. From left to right: Irv Noren, me, and Billy Martin. August 27, 1952.

Left to right: *top*, Yogi Berra, me; *bottom*, Allie Reynolds and Vic Raschi.

We win the 1952 World Series from the Dodgers. Left to right: me, Bob Kuzava, and Gene Woodling. The score: 4–2.

I pop to Peewee Reese.

I ground to Hodges.

I homer. It's hard to tell from these photographs which was the successful hit and which wasn't. They look alike to me.

The last Yankee Stadium shower of the year. It's a great feeling after your team has won the World Series.

ASSOCIATED PRESS PHOTO

Mama and Merlyn pose for a last picture before taking off for Commerce, Oklahoma.

INTERNATIONAL NEWS PHOTOS

Merlyn and my sister-in-law, Patty Johnson, dip into the scrapbook.